Reproducible Activities

Brain Games
Mind-Stretching Classroom Activities

Grades 4-5

By
Delana Heidrich

Cover Design by
Peggy Jackson

Published by Instructional Fair • TS Denison
an imprint of

About the Author
Delana Heidrich has a number of published professional resource books for social studies and language arts teachers. She also facilitates home-schooling seminars and presents creative writing workshops at Klamath Community College in Klamath Falls, Oregon. Delana spends much of her time tutoring disabled middle school students. She currently teaches in Bonanza, Oregon, where she lives with her family. She received both bachelor's and master's degrees from Dominican College in San Rafael, California, and has since earned an advanced degree in educational curriculum and instruction.

Credits
Author: Delana Heidrich
Cover Design: Peggy Jackson
Project Director/Editor: Jerry Aten
Editors: Jeanine Manfro, Alyson Kieda, Kathryn Wheeler
Page Design: Peggy Jackson
Page Production: Lentz Design, C.J. Designs, Wayne Newton

McGraw-Hill Children's Publishing

A Division of The McGraw-Hill Companies

Published by Instructional Fair • TS Denison
An imprint of McGraw-Hill Children's Publishing
Copyright © 2002 McGraw-Hill Children's Publishing

Limited Reproduction Permission: Permission to duplicate these materials is limited to the person for whom they are purchased. Reproduction for an entire school or school district is unlawful and strictly prohibited.

Send all inquiries to:
McGraw-Hill Children's Publishing
3195 Wilson Drive NW
Grand Rapids, Michigan 49544

All Rights Reserved • Printed in the United States of America

Brain Games—grades 4–5
ISBN: 0-7424-0212-6

1 2 3 4 5 6 7 8 9 07 06 05 04 03 02

Table of Contents

Games for Individuals

Get Out of Here—6

Triangle Trouble—13

Triple Word Search—19

Delving into Directions—25

Mixed Messages—31

Black Out Boxes—38

Partner Games

You're Out of Order—45

Dictionary Detective—51

Drop in the Bucket—58

Look It Up—70

Four-Minute Fury—76

Matching Madness—82

Games for the Entire Class

Five Minutes Flat—89

Speak Your Mind—95

Know Your Neighbor—101

Let Me Explain—107

Story Add-Ons—113

Sentence Sense—119

Ask the Experts—125

To the Teacher

The music teacher says he will be ten minutes late in arriving in your classroom today; a small group of students finishes a project early; or your best reader completes her literature assignment ahead of the class again. Don't panic! There is no reason learners need to be bored or disruptive when they discover a few "free" minutes. **BRAIN GAMES** can engage your students in challenging and fun brain-stretching exercises while they await the start of the next lesson.

BRAIN GAMES is divided into these three main sections: ***Games for Individuals***, ***Partner Games***, and ***Games for the Entire Class***. Activities in the ***Games for Individuals*** and ***Partner Games*** sections are designed to allow students who finish work early to play educational games without the assistance of a teacher. ***Games for the Entire Class*** were created to engage your whole class in meaningful activities led by either a teacher or student.

Games in each section are divided into four- to six-game series. Each game series contains a one-page ***instructions card*** and four or more ***game cards***. The ***instructions card*** tells students about the goal and the rules of the game and lists any common classroom materials necessary for play. This card should be attached to the front of the file folder that will store game sheets for play. Answers to all games in a series are printed in an ***answer key*** that should be attached to the back of the folder. The ***game cards*** correspond to the subject areas of language arts, math, social studies, science, and sometimes extracurricular activities. The game card includes descriptions, samples, game boards, or information necessary to play the game.

Preparing for play with **BRAIN GAMES** is easy:
1. Make one copy of the ***instructions card*** from each series. Attach the card to the front of a file folder and attach the ***answer key*** to the the back of the folder.
2. Reproduce numerous copies of all ***game cards*** from each series. Since the cards will be cut apart and written on, students will discard ***game cards*** after use.
3. When students wish to play a game, they simply choose one of the folders and read the instructions on how to play the game on the front the folder. They then choose whatever game card they wish to use and they are ready to begin play.
4. When play has been completed, players may wish to check the accuracy of their answers by returning to the folder to check the ***answer key***.

Store a stack of ***Games for Individuals*** and ***Partner Games*** in the back of your classroom where students can go to exercise their brains when they finish any activity early. Keep a stack of ***Games for the Entire Class*** on your desk for play anytime.

Instructions

Get Out of Here

Players: One

Materials: Game card, pencil

Goal: Find the word or phrase that does not fit in each group of words or phrases. Then discover what the discarded words all have in common.

Rules:
1. Select a *Get Out of Here* game card.
2. Circle the word, phrase, or numbers that do not fit in each problem on the card.
3. In the space provided write why the word, phrase, or number does not fit.
4. Answer the question at the bottom of the card that asks what all the circled words, phrases, or numbers have in common.
5. Check your answers with the *Get Out of Here* answer key on the back of the game folder.

Answer Key
Get Out of Here

Science Similarities

Circled Word	Because Word Is Not...	Circled Word	Because Word Is Not...
1. microscope	a type of glasses	2. rats	a reptile
3. test tube	used for drinking	4. scientist	a salesperson
5. chemicals	a metal	6. thermometer	a temperature
7. lab coat	exercise clothes	8. safety goggles	winter clothes
9. eye dropper	a facial feature	10. funnel	used for storage
11. magnet	a metal fastener	12. compass	a clock
13. ruler	for measuring volume	14. lab book	a type of chart
15. magnifying glass	a type of net		

What do the circled words have in common? They can all be found in a science laboratory.

Common to the Culture

Circled Word	Because Word Is Not...	Circled Word	Because Word Is Not...
1. corn	a fruit	2. feathers	a bird
3. buffalo	a fish	4. bow and arrow	a land feature
5. totem pole	a plant	6. tepee	furniture
7. chief	a military rank	8. war paint	for hair care
9. basket	a dish	10. dream catcher	a type of dream
11. rain dance	a visual art	12. pottery	silverware
13. drum	a brass instrument	14. beads	a fastener
15. leather	a farm animal		

What do the circled words have in common? They are all part of Native American culture.

It All Adds Up

Circled Word	Because Solution Is Not...	Circled Word	Because Solution Is Not...
1. 2 + 4	an odd number	2. 87 + 1	divisible by 10
3. 18 + 1	divisible by 4	4. $1\frac{3}{4} + 2\frac{1}{3}$	a whole number
5. 1 + 2	a product	6. 24 + 32	a single-digit number
7. 52 + 33	an even number	8. 23 + 3	showing a 3 in last digit
9. $3\frac{1}{4} + 2\frac{3}{4}$	a mixed number	10. 6.5 + 2.5	a decimal
11. 17 + 7	a dividend	12. 100 + 72	a two-digit number
13. 23 + 4	a prime number	14. 32 + 4	showing a 2 in first digit
15. 41 + 3	showing a 1 in every digit		

What do the circled equations have in common? They are all addition problems.

Note: Other answers are possible, but would change the outcome: not all circled equations would be addition problems.

Answer Key: Get Out of Here (continued)

Telling Stories

Circled Word	Because Word Is Not...	Circled Word	Because Word Is Not...
1. setting	a place	2. plot	a type of story
3. characters	a name	4. climax	a landform
5. chapters	a ranking	6. conflict	a solution
7. genre	a type of story	8. growth	meaning to get smaller
9. theme	a recreational place	10. resolution	a dispute
11. irony	meaning to question	12. dialect	a region
13. symbol	an American symbol	14. moral	a mentor
15. narrator	a movie industry employee		

What do the circled words have in common? They are all words related to literature.

Reasons why circled words do not fit may vary.

Name_____ Date_____

Science Similarities

Circle the word or phrase that does not fit in each line and tell why.

Words and Phrases

Circled Word
Does Not Fit,
Because It Is Not…

1. microscope   sunglasses   reading glasses   bifocals   _____
2. lizards   rats   snakes   turtles   _____
3. coffee mug   tea cup   juice glass   test tube   _____
4. grocery clerk   scientist   real estate agent   car salesman   _____
5. gold   silver   copper   chemicals   _____
6. thermometer   cold   hot   warm   _____
7. t-shirt   lab coat   sweat pants   jogging shoes   _____
8. hat   gloves   safety goggles   scarf   _____
9. eye dropper   nose   mouth   chin   _____
10. box   funnel   bag   basket   _____
11. nail   tack   pin   magnet   _____
12. alarm clock   compass   cuckoo clock   watch   _____
13. ruler   teaspoon   tablespoon   measuring cup   _____
14. chart   lab book   graph   diagram   _____
15. butterfly net   hair net   magnifying glass   fishnet   _____

What do all the words you circled have in common?

_____

Name_____ Date_____

Common to the Culture

Circle the word or phrase that does not fit in each line and tell why.

Words and Phrases

Circled Word
Does Not Fit,
Because It Is Not...

1.	corn	apple	banana	orange	_____
2.	feathers	chicken	turkey	duck	_____
3.	salmon	trout	catfish	buffalo	_____
4.	river	mountain	bow and arrow	valley	_____
5.	tree	totem pole	bush	flower	_____
6.	tepee	chair	couch	table	_____
7.	colonel	chief	lieutenant	private	_____
8.	comb	war paint	barrette	hair tie	_____
9.	cup	bowl	plate	basket	_____
10.	nightmare	dream	dream catcher	daydream	_____
11.	rain dance	painting	sculpture	collage	_____
12.	fork	knife	pottery	spoon	_____
13.	drum	trumpet	tuba	trombone	_____
14.	buttons	beads	zipper	snap	_____
15.	cow	horse	donkey	leather	_____

What do all the words you circled have in common?

_____

© McGraw-Hill Children's Publishing   IF87061 *Brain Games*

It All Adds Up

Circle the equation whose solution is unlike the other solutions in each set. Then tell why the circled equation does not fit.

Equations

Circled Equation Does Not Fit, Because Its Solution Is Not…

1.	1 x 3 =	2 + 4 =	9 – 2 =	72 – 1 =	_____
2.	9 + 1 =	37 + 3 =	87 + 1 =	⁻9 + 1 =	_____
3.	8 x 2 =	8 x 3 =	18 + 1 =	19 + 1 =	_____
4.	$1\frac{1}{2} + 2\frac{1}{2} =$	$1\frac{3}{4} + 2\frac{1}{3} =$	9 x 1 =	14 ÷ 7 =	_____
5.	1 + 2 =	2 x 3 =	4 x 5 =	6 x 7 =	_____
6.	64 ÷ 8 =	24 + 32 =	7 x 1 =	3 + 6 =	_____
7.	2 + 4 =	6 x 3 =	24 ÷ 6 =	52 + 33 =	_____
8.	3 x 11 =	23 + 3 =	50 + 3 =	87 – 4 =	_____
9.	$3\frac{1}{4} + 2\frac{3}{4} =$	$1\frac{1}{2} + 1\frac{1}{4} =$	$4\frac{1}{8} + 5 =$	$5\frac{1}{6} + 3 =$	_____
10.	1.5 x 1.7 =	3.5 x 3 =	4.7 + 5 =	6.5 + 2.5 =	_____
11.	12 ÷ 2 =	24 ÷ 6 =	17 + 7 =	40 ÷ 5 =	_____
12.	12 x 2 =	100 - 53 =	100 + 72 =	48 ÷ 2 =	_____
13.	14 ÷ 2 =	1 x 3 =	23 + 4 =	16 + 1 =	_____
14.	66 ÷ 3 =	32 + 4 =	30 – 2 =	10 x 2 =	_____
15.	10 + 1 =	150 – 39 =	41 + 3 =	7 – 6 =	_____

What do all the equations you circled have in common?

_____

Name_____ Date_____

Language Arts
Get Out of Here

Telling Stories

Circle the word or phrase that does not fit in each line and tell why.

Words and Phrases				Circled Word Does Not Fit, Because It is Not...
1. desert	setting	beach	city	_____
2. plot	play	short story	novel	_____
3. Bill	Sam	Tom	characters	_____
4. climax	mountain	hill	cliff	_____
5. first	second	chapters	third	_____
6. conflict	agreement	compromise	contract	_____
7. western	genre	romance	fantasy	_____
8. shrinking	decreasing	reducing	growth	_____
9. theme	amusement park	playground	skating rink	_____
10. fight	resolution	argument	disagreement	_____
11. ask	inquire	question	irony	_____
12. dialect	The South	France	New York	_____
13. flag	red, white, and blue	symbol	Uncle Sam	_____
14. moral	teacher	instructor	coach	_____
15. actor	narrator	director	producer	_____

What do all the words you circled have in common?
_____

Instructions
Triangle Trouble

Players: One

Materials: Game card, pencil

Goal: Create words by choosing the correct letters from the triangles presented.

Rules:
1. Select a game card from the *Triangle Trouble* series.
2. For each problem on the card, select one letter from each triangle to create a word that fits the theme of the page.
3. Write the words on the spaces provided.
4. Check your answers with the *Triangle Trouble* answer key on the back of the game folder.

Spaced Out:
1. PLANETS
2. STARS
3. PLUTO
4. MARS
5. VENUS
6. SUN
7. MERCURY
8. EARTH
9. URANUS
10. JUPITER

Presenting the Presidents:
1. MONROE
2. JEFFERSON
3. BUSH
4. HOOVER
5. REAGAN
6. LINCOLN
7. POLK
8. WILSON
9. KENNEDY
10. NIXON

Shaping Up:
1. TRIANGLE
2. RECTANGLE
3. CIRCLE
4. SQUARE
5. HEXAGON
6. STAR
7. DIAMOND
8. OCTAGON
9. PENTAGON
10. TRAPEZOID

Musical Moods:
1. ROCK
2. RAP
3. REGGAE
4. CLASSICAL
5. OPERA
6. POP
7. NEW AGE
8. BLUEGRASS
9. SYMPHONIC
10. COUNTRY

Triangle Trouble

Spaced Out

Select one letter from each triangle to create a word that names a planet or fits the general theme of outer space.

1. PLANETS
2. STARS
3. PLUTO
4. MARS
5. VENUS
6. SUN
7. MERCURY
8. EARTH
9. URANUS
10. JUPITER

Presenting the Presidents

Create the last names of past American presidents by choosing one letter from each of the triangles below.

1. J P M O O E / M H, O N, S N, U R, V W, X N _____
2. R E W F S O K O U / J J, M N, F H, N R, M E, R B, S V, A T, I N _____
3. B K S C / M S, R U, B D, H L _____
4. C D Y W J R / H S, T O, O M, S V, E K, M N _____
5. R M J T M S / S W, E P, A Q, R G, Q A, N V _____
6. C I N C R W A / A L, E G, J M, O P, O U, L Y, N E _____
7. P L R S / E A, O M, N L, K E _____
8. A I P S Z J / O W, L M, L Q, U R, T O, K N _____
9. B E N F E D L / K Q, R T, L P, N J, M T, Q R, Y S _____
10. G I V P D / M N, S T, X R, J O, L N _____

© McGraw-Hill Children's Publishing   IF87061 *Brain Games*

Shaping Up!
For each problem, select one letter from each triangle to create a word that names a shape. Shapes may be two- or three-dimensional.

1. TRIANGLE
2. RECTANGLE
3. CIRCLE
4. SQUARE
5. HEXAGON
6. STAR
7. DIAMOND
8. OCTAGON
9. PENTAGON
10. TRAPEZOID

Name _____ **Date** _____

Music: Triangle Trouble

Musical Moods

Select one letter from each triangle to form a word that names a different type of music.

 1. _____

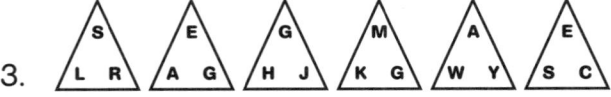 2. _____

 3. _____

4. _____

 5. _____

 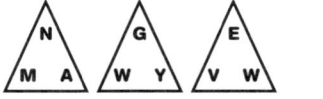 6. _____

7. _____

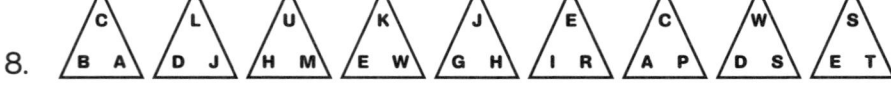 8. _____

 9. _____

 10. _____

© McGraw-Hill Children's Publishing   IF87061 Brain Games

Instructions
Triple Word Search

Players: One

Materials: Game card, pencil, (atlas and thesaurus optional)

Goal: Locate words in three types of puzzles and guess what they all have in common.

Rules:
1. Choose a game card from the *Triple Word Search* series.
2. In Part A, locate and circle the words listed below the word search box. Words may be shown backwards, forwards, up, down, or diagonally in the puzzle.
3. In Part B, rearrange the letters in the given word or words to create 6 new words. Be certain the words you create contain 3 or more letters each.
4. In Part C, unscramble the letters presented to create words.
5. Decide what all of the words presented in Parts A, B, and C have in common. In your answer, do not consider the words you created from the given word in Part B.
6. Check your answers with the *Triple Word Search* answer key on the back of the game folder.

Answer Key
Triple Word Search

(Note: Answers will vary in Part B for all games in this series. Any three- or more-letter word that includes letters from the presented word is acceptable.

Flip the Switch:
Part A:

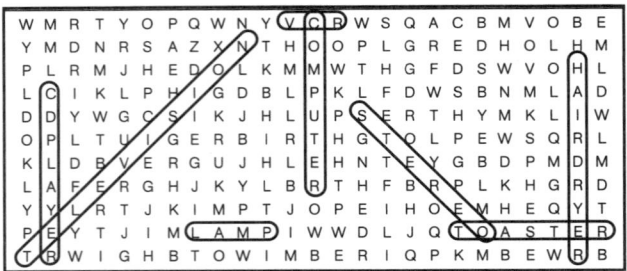

Part C:
1. microwave
2. refrigerator
3. clock
4. coffee maker
5. vacuum
6. curling iron

What do all of the words have in common?
They are electrical household appliances.

Where in the World?:
Part A:

Part C:
1. France
2. India
3. United States
4. China
5. Japan
6. Australia

What do all of the words have in common?
They are names of countries.

How Much? How Many?:
Part A:

Part C:
1. gallon
2. cup
3. meter
4. Celsius
5. yard
6. pint

What do all of the words have in common?
They are measurements.

Speaking of Which:
Part A:

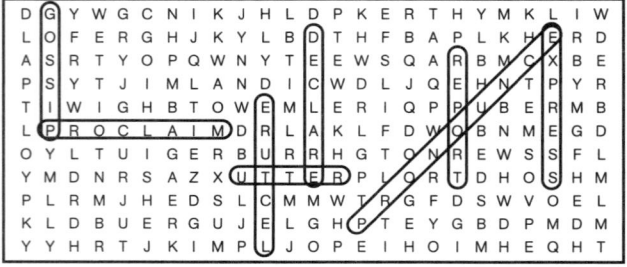

Part C:
1. speak
2. say
3. tell
4. discuss
5. chat
6. remark

What do all of the words have in common?
They are synonyms for "talk."

© McGraw-Hill Children's Publishing   IF87061 Brain Games

Triple Word Search

Flip the Switch

Part A: Find and circle the words listed below.

```
W M R T Y O P Q W N Y V C R W S Q A C B M V O B E
Y M D N R S A Z X N T H O O P L G R E D H O L H M
P L R M J H E D O L K M M W T H G F D S W V O H L
L C I K L P H I G D B L P K L F D W S B N M L A D
D D Y W G C S I K J H L U P S E R T H Y M K L I W
O P L T U I G E R B I R T H G T O L P E W S Q R L
K L D B V E R G U J H L E H N T E Y G B D P M D M
L A F E R G H J K Y L B R T H F B R P L K H G R D
Y Y L R T J K I M P T J O P E I H O E M H E Q Y T
P E Y T J I M L A M P I W W D L J Q T O A S T E R
T R W I G H B T O W I M B E R I Q P K M B E W R B
```

television   stereo   toaster   VCR
CD player   lamp   computer   hair dryer

Part B: Use letters from the words below to create new words:
SEWING MACHINE

_____ _____ _____

_____ _____ _____

_____ _____ _____

Part C: Unscramble the words:

1. civwormae _____   4. fofeec kamre _____

2. otrfiarererg _____   5. cuuavm _____

3. olckc _____   6. rilnguc nroi _____

What do all the words have in common? _____

Name _____ Date _____

Where in the World?

Part A: Find and circle the words listed below.

```
A R G I E C A I S M B G B E L G I U M A L O B E B
N B S S A N I T N E G R A K F T K T U Q T R D J U
L A N D T E I F H B B X N A S B E N W D X I T N R
B F I B O J P N T D Y L G Z U I A I S V R C F F N
N E T H E R L A N D S R L S R W I N S R H U C T A
T I Y Q T H Y A D T I T A L Y N Q B A B U R M A D
B E R S Z K L I V U L P D X G R M J U W V M A W N
J A O M D N T S E G T B E M V S R L N A S N V O A
D A S D I A G B O O B P S C B O T S O A D T S U L
S I W F V P Z I N E T H H G Q E S H G S Y O O J I
P S E R T H Y M K L B E L U L F D F I E D P F B F
```

    Netherlands   Bangladesh   Belgium   Burma
    Argentina   Finland   Italy   Botswana

Part B: Use letters from the word below to create new words:
SWITZERLAND

_____ _____ _____

_____ _____ _____

_____ _____ _____

Part C: Unscramble the words. Capitalize proper nouns:

1. rncaef _____   4. acinh   _____

2. aidni   _____   5. paajn   _____

3. nutide tatsse _____   6. aatlusiar _____

What do all the words have in common? _____

Name_____ Date_____

Triple Word Search

How Much? How Many?

Part A: Find and circle the words listed below.

```
L D F E R G H J K Y L B H T H F B A P L K H G R D
A I R T Y O P Q W N Y T N P W S Q A C B M V O B E
P S T T J I M L A N D I W O D L J Q T H A T N Y R
P L R E J H E D N L K M Q U A R T M A R G V O E L
L B I K R P H I O D B L P N L F D I S B N M L G D
D D Y W G C T I O J H L D D K E R L H Y M K L I W
O Y L T U O G E P B I R T H G T O E P E W H Q F L
Y M D N O S A Z S M T H F O P L G R E D H O C H M
K L D F U E R G A J H L G H N T E Y G B D P M N M
Y Y H R T J K I E P T J O P E I H O I M H E Q H I
T R W I G H B T T W I M B E R I Q P K M B E W M B
```

    teaspoon   liter   inch   pound
    gram   mile   quart   foot

Part B: Use letters from the word below to create new words:
TABLESPOON

_____   _____   _____

_____   _____   _____

Part C: Unscramble the words. Capitalize proper nouns:

1. lolagn _____   4. ssileuc _____

2. pcu _____   5. rday _____

3. teerm _____   6. nipt _____

What do all the words have in common? _____

© McGraw-Hill Children's Publishing   **23**   IF87061 *Brain Games*

Name _____ Date _____

Language Arts
Triple Word Search

Speaking of Which

Part A: Find and circle the words listed below.

```
D G Y W G C N I K J H L D P K E R T H Y M K L I W
L O F E R G H J K Y L B D T H F B A P L K H E R D
A S R T Y O P Q W N Y T E E W S Q A R B M C X B E
P S Y T J I M L A N D I C W D L J Q E H N T P Y R
T I W I G H B T O W E M L E R I Q P P U B E R M B
L P R O C L A I M D R L A K L F D W O B N M E G D
O Y L T U I G E R B U R R H G T O N R E W S S F L
Y M D N R S A Z X U T T E R P L O R T D H O S H M
P L R M J H E D S L C M M W T R G F D S W V O E L
K L D B U E R G U J E L G H P T E Y G B D P M D M
Y Y H R T J K I M P L J O P E I H O I M H E Q H T
```

gossip   utter   declare   report
lecture   proclaim   express   pronounce

Part B: Create new words from the word below:
CONVERSATION

_____   _____   _____

_____   _____   _____

_____   _____   _____

Part C: Unscramble the words:

1. pksea _____   4. ssscuid _____

2. ysa _____   5. htac _____

3. ltel _____   6. mreark _____

What do all the words have in common? _____

© McGraw-Hill Children's Publishing   **24**   IF87061 *Brain Games*

Instructions
Delving into Directions

Players: One

Materials: Game cards, unlined paper, pencil, five nickels, paperback novel, textbook, scissors, calculator

Goal: Follow directions to complete a task.

Rules:
1. Select a game card from the *Delving into Directions* series.
2. Follow the directions on the game card exactly. Different cards will lead you through experiments, map reading, word and number converting, or paper-craft creating.
3. Answer the questions presented about what you discovered in completing each set of instructions.
4. Check your answers with the *Delving into Directions* answer key on the back of the game folder.

Surprising Science:
Question 1: The nickel at the far end of the line of nickels shoots forward from the momentum sent through the line by the flicked nickel.
Question 2: The book balances because you have found its center of gravity.
Question 3: Objects fall at the same speed regardless of their weight.
Question 4: The paper sticks to the wall for a short time due to the electricity produced by friction as you rubbed your hand on the paper.

Where Did Sam Go?:
A. home
B. baseball field
C. home, Performing Arts Center
D. babysitter's house, home
E. candy store, home

Math Magic:
A. the digits are reversed
B. it is the same
C. goose
D. "Hello"

Sentence Swapping:
A: School begins at _____.
               (time school begins for you)
B. My favorite sport is _____.
               (your favorite sport)

Name_____ Date_____

Delving into Directions

SURPRISING SCIENCE
Follow the directions exactly to discover some science surprises.

Money in Motion:
1. Locate five nickels.
2. Lay four of the nickels on a table or desk in a straight line. The nickels should be touching each other.
3. Place the fifth nickel about two inches away from the last nickel in your line of nickels.
4. Flick the nickel that is not touching the other nickels toward the line of nickels.

Question One: What happens when the flicked nickel hits the last nickel in your line of nickels?

Book Balancing:
1. Curl the four fingers of your right hand in to make a fist.
2. Raise your right thumb into the air.
3. Place a paperback novel on your outstretched thumb. Move it around until the book balances on your thumb.

Question Two: Why does the book balance on your thumb?

Gravity's Greatness:
1. Stand up.
2. Hold a heavy textbook in your left hand and a pencil in your right.
3. Stretch both of your arms straight out in front of you.
4. Drop the book and the pencil from your hands at the same instant.

Question Three: What conclusion can you make by noticing when the pencil and book hit the floor?

Sticky Situation:
1. Cut a sheet of paper in half lengthwise.
2. Hold one of the resulting strips in your hand horizontally.
3. Cut the strip in half from bottom to top. You should now have one long strip of paper and two smaller rectangles.
4. Carry one of the rectangles to the nearest smooth wall or window.
5. Hold the paper rectangle to the wall or window with you left hand.
6. Rub the paper rectangle with your right hand several times.

Question Four: What happens when you let go of the paper rectangle with both hands?

Name_____   Date_____

Social Studies
Delving into Directions

Where Did Sam Go?

Use the map and follow the directions provided to fill in the blanks about where Sam went after school each day last week.

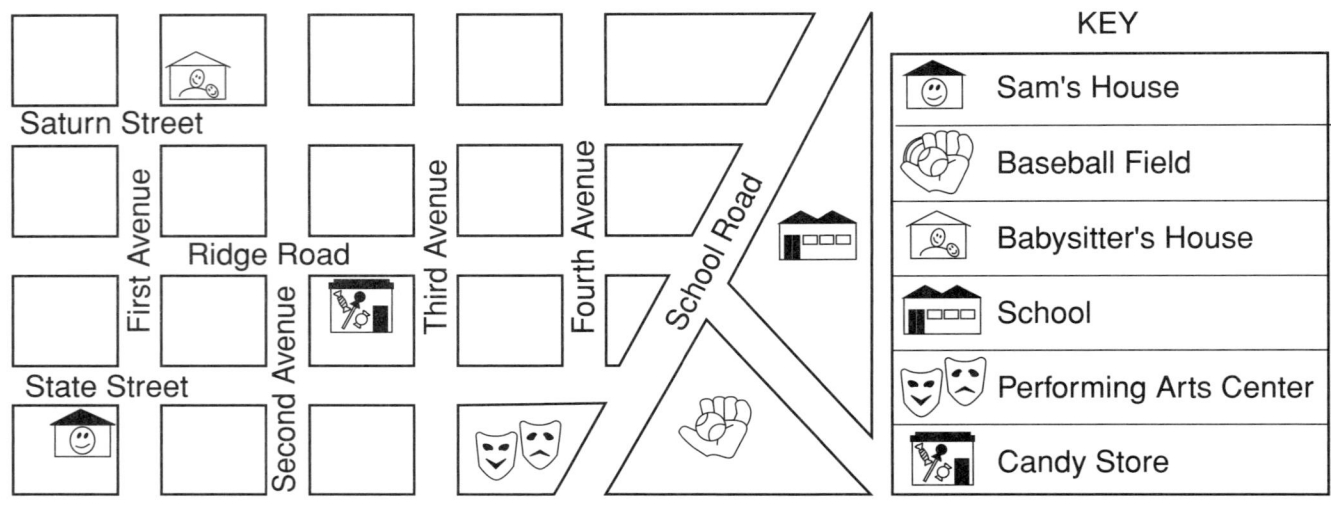

A. On Monday, Sam walked 4 blocks west on Ridge Road. He turned left on First Avenue, and walked 2 more blocks. Finally Sam was _____.

B. On Tuesday, Sam walked southwest on School Road until he got to the _____ on the same side of the street as the school itself.

C. On Wednesday, Sam walked 4 blocks west on Ridge Road. He turned left on First Avenue, and walked 2 more blocks. Sam entered his _____ and grabbed a snack. Then he ran out the door and 3 blocks east on State Street. He entered the side door of the _____ just in time for dance lessons.

D. On Thursday, Sam walked 4 blocks west on Saturn Street until he reached his little sister's _____. He and his sister left through the side gate and walked 3 blocks south on First Street until they were _____.

E. On Friday, Sam walked 2 blocks west on Ridge Road until the reached the _____. He bought a piece of candy for himself and one for his sister. Then he walked out the store's south entrance and 2 blocks west to make his way _____.

© McGraw-Hill Children's Publishing   IF87061 *Brain Games*

Name _____ Date _____

Math Magic
Follow the directions below and answer the questions about what you discover.

A. Begin with the number 348.
    Add 58.
    Divide by 4.
    Multiply by 2.
    Add 78.
    Multiply by 3.
How does your answer compare with your beginning number? _____

B. Begin with your age.
    Multiply by 2.
    Add 10.
    Divide by 2.
    Subtract 5.
How does your answer compare with your age? _____

C. Use a calculator for this one.
    Begin with the number 95.
    Multiply by the square root of 36.
    Add 3,000.
    Multiply by 4 squared.
    Divide by 2.
    Add 6446.
What farm animal appears in the window of your calculator when you turn it upside-down? _____

D. Use a calculator for this one too. As you read the story below, add all the distances Kim travels to catch up with her friend, Edward. Remember to convert fractions to decimals since you will be adding on a calculator.

    Kim walked a $\frac{1}{2}$ mile to her friend Edward's house to deliver a message. Edward was not home. Kim decided to try the park. She walked a $\frac{1}{4}$ mile from Edward's house to the park. From the edge of the park, she could see her friend standing beside the tennis court. She only had to walk 0.0234 of a mile more to catch up with Edward. When she did, she gave him the message.

Turn your calculator over to read the message Kim had for Edward: _____

Language Arts: Delving into Directions

Sentence Swapping

Follow the directions presented to turn the questions below into answers.

A. What time does school begin?

    1. Swap the first and fourth words in the question.

    2. Swap the second and fifth words in your new question.

    3. Add an s to the second word in your new question.

    4. Drop the third word from your new question.

    5. Drop the first two letters of the third word from your new question.

    6. Replace the word **time** with the actual time your school begins.

    7. Replace the question mark at the end of your new question with a period.

B. What is your favorite sport?

    1. Replace the word **your** with the word **my** in the question.

    2. Move the word **what** to the end of your new question.

    3. Move the first word of your new question to the position right before the word **what**.

    4. Replace the last word of your new question with the name of your favorite sport.

    5. Replace the question mark at the end of your new question with a period.

Instructions

Mixed Messages

Players: One

Materials: Game card, scissors

Goal: Unscramble mixed messages.

Rules:
1. Select a game card from the *Mixed Messages* series.
2. Read the Theme Statement at the top of the page.
   Part A: True statements relating to the theme are presented in mixed-up order.
   1. Cut Statement One out.
   2. Then cut along the dashed lines to divide the words in Statement One.
   3. Now move the words around until you have created a reasonable sentence.
   4. Repeat the process with each statement.
   5. Check your answers with the *Mixed Messages* answer key on the back of the game folder.

   Part B: True statements relating to the theme are presented with word breaks in the wrong places.
   1. Attempt to read the statements aloud several times in order to find where one word should end and another should begin.
   2. Rewrite the sentences correctly on the spaces provided.
   3. Check your answers with the *Mixed Messages* answer key on the back of the game folder.

Answer Key: Mixed Messages

New Ideas:

Part A:
1. The inventor of rayon was trying to make a substitute for silk.
2. The postage stamp was invented by Roland Hill in 1840.
3. The first tea bags were made of silk.

Part B:
1. Glass drinking straws were used by ancient Greeks and Romans.
2. A popular beverage was named after a football team called the "Gators."
3. The inventor of Jello® had trouble convincing people to try his new product.
4. Games using cards, dice, and dominoes are ancient.
5. A geography teacher invented the jigsaw puzzle to teach his students about maps.

American Patriots:

Part A:
1. Cesar Chavez organized farmers into the United Farm Workers Union.
2. Susan B. Anthony worked for the right of women to vote.
3. A former slave named Robert Smalls served three terms in the United States House of Representatives.

Part B:
1. The first United States patent was granted to Samuel Hopkins of Vermont.
2. President Calvin Coolidge declared Father's Day a national holiday.
3. Benjamin Franklin was a talented inventor, statesman, and diplomat.
4. James Audubon published writings and drawings related to his studies of birds.
5. Jim Thorpe excelled in baseball, football, and track.

Answer Key: Mixed Messages (continued)

Number Geniuses:

Part A: 1. The Greek philosopher, Pythagoras, wrote a rule about right triangles. Or, Pythagoras, the Greek philosopher, wrote a rule about right triangles.
2. Sections of a math textbook written by Euclid around 300 B.C. are still used in geometry classes today.
3. Qin Jinshao was a famous Chinese mathematician who lived during the thirteenth century.

Part B: 1. Einstein once failed a math class.
2. Galileo was a mathematician and scientist who studied motion and gravity.
3. Blaise Pascal suggested famous geometry theories before the age of sixteen.
4. Sir Isaac Newton invented calculus.

Amazing Authors:

Part A: 1. John Ciardi was a famous modern poet in America.
2. In 1644, Anne Bradstreet became the first published poet in America.
3. Dr. Seuss's real name was Theodore Geisel.
4. Laura Ingalls Wilder did not begin writing until she was in her sixties.

Part B: 1. As a child, Charles Dickens worked in a factory to help support his family.
2. Lewis Carroll, who wrote *Alice in Wonderland*, was a mathematician.
3. E.B. White, author of *Charlotte's Web*, was born in 1899.
4. Hans Christian Andersen wrote famous fairy tales including *The Ugly Duckling*.

Name_____ Date_____

New Ideas

Theme Statement: The mixed-up messages below tell about inventions and inventors.

PART A: Unscramble the messages.

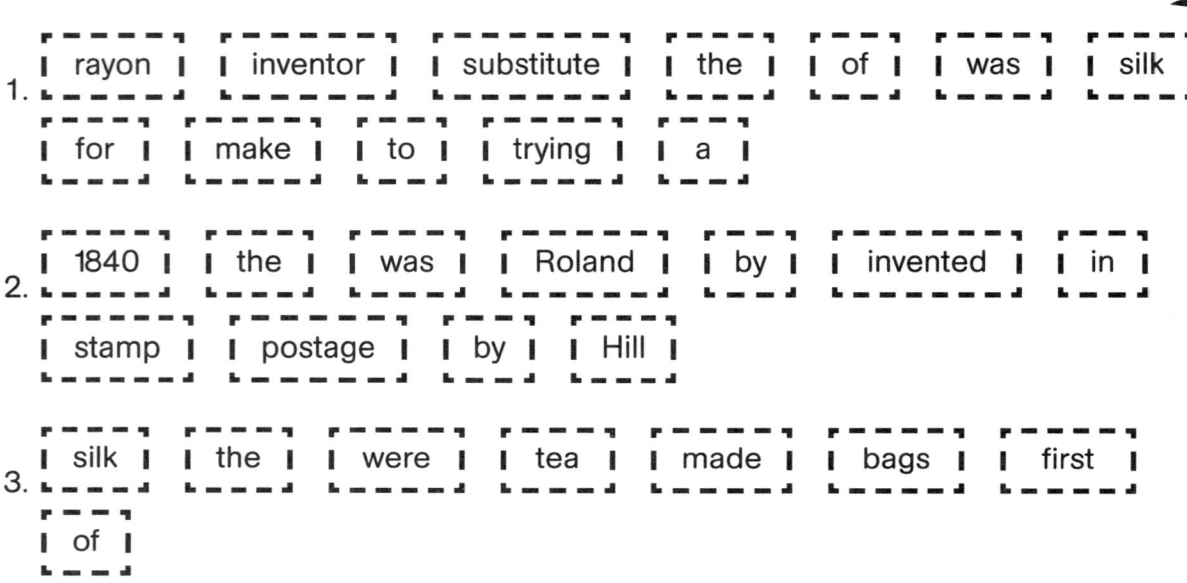

PART B: Rewrite the sentences by breaking words at the correct places and adding necessary punctuation and capitalization.

1. Gla ssdri nkin gstra wsw ereu sedbyan cien tgre eksan dro mans.
_____

2. Apop ul arbev era gewa sname daft erafo otb all tea mcal ledt he"Gat ors."
_____

3. Theinven torofJe llo®hadtr oublec onvinc ingpe opleto tryh isnewp roduct.
_____

4. Game susin gcar dsd ice an ddom inoes arean cie nt.
_____

5. Age ograph y tea cher in vent edth ejig saw puz zlet otea chhi sstu dentsa b out ma ps.
_____

© McGraw-Hill Children's Publishing

Name _____   Date _____

Social Studies

Mixed Messages

American Patriots

Theme Statement: The mixed-up messages below tell about the accomplishments of American citizens who have made a positive contribution to the United States.

PART A: Unscramble the sentences.

1. | Workers | | organized | | into | | farmers | | Cesar | | Union |
| Farm | | the | | Chavez | | United |

2. | Anthony | | the | | vote | | to | | B. | | worked | | right |
| women | | of | | Susan | | for |

3. | named | | former | | three | | Smalls | | United | | of |
| slave | | Representatives | | Robert | | terms | | served |
| States | | A | | the | | House | | in |

PART B: Rewrite the sentences by breaking words at the correct places and adding necessary punctuation and capitalization.

1. Thefi rst un ite dstat espat entwas grant edto sam uel hɔpk in sofverm ont.
_____

2. Pres id entcal vin cool id gede clar edfa the r'sda yana tio nalh oli day.
_____

3. Ben jam in fran klinw asata lent edin vent or state sma nandd iplo mat.
_____

4. Jam esau dubo npub lish edwrit ing sand draw ingsr elate dto hi sstu die sofb irds.
_____

5. Jimth orpeex cell edin bas eba llfo otb all andtr ack.
_____

© McGraw-Hill Children's Publishing   35   IF87061 *Brain Games*

Name_____ Date_____

Number Geniuses

Theme Statement: The mixed-up messages below tell about the lives of famous mathematicians.

PART A: Unscramble the sentences.

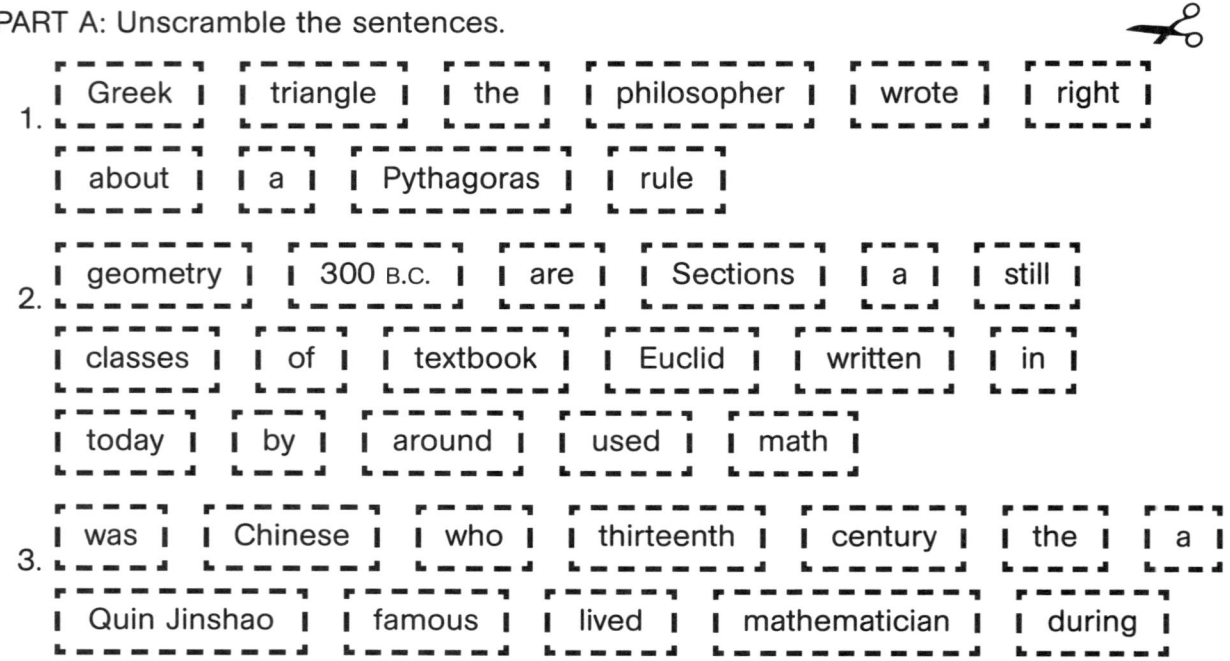

PART B: Rewrite the sentences by breaking words at the correct places and adding necessary punctuation and capitalization.

1. Ein ste in on cef ail edam athc lass.

_____

2. Ga lil eow asam athe maticia nand sci enti stwhost udie dmo tiona ndgr av ity.

_____

3. Bla isePa sca lsug geste dfam ousge ome try the oriesb efo rethe ageo fsix teen.

_____

4. S irls aacN ew ton in vente dcalc ul us.

_____

Amazing Authors

Theme Statement: The mixed-up messages below tell about the lives of famous authors.

PART A: Unscramble the sentences.

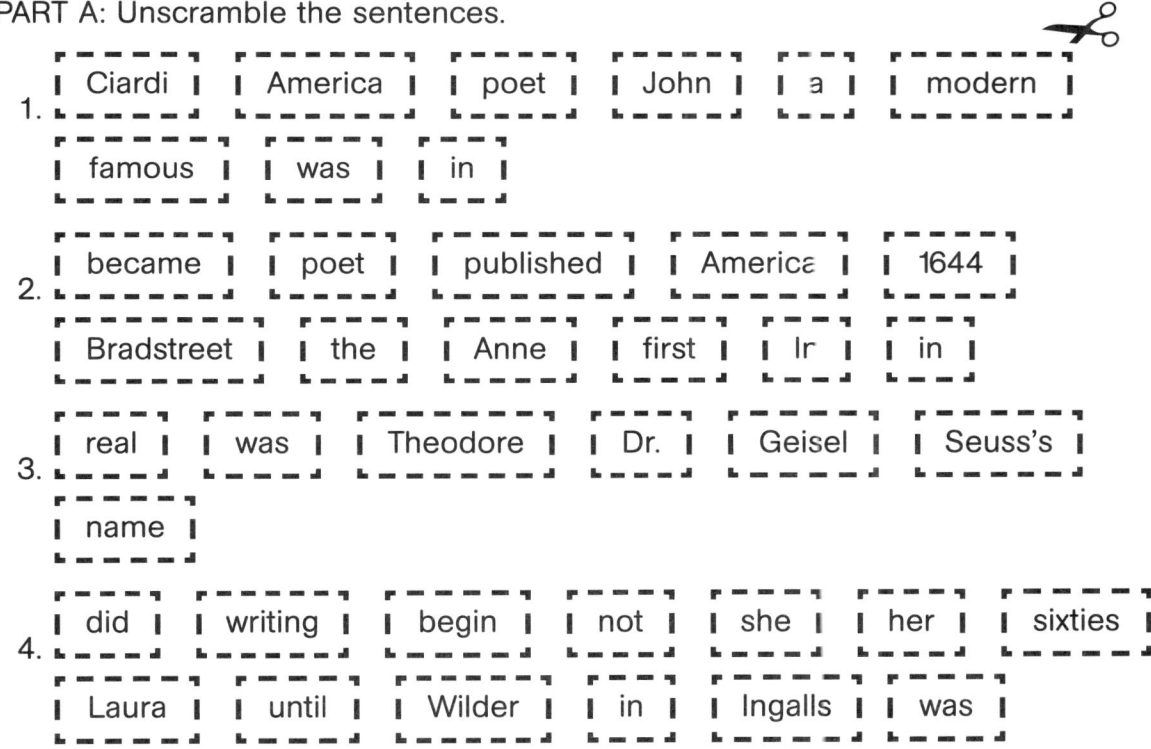

PART B: Rewrite the sentences by breaking the words at the correct places and adding necessary punctuation and capitalization.

1. Asa chil dchar lesdi ck enswo rkedin afa ctoryt ohe lpsup porth isfam ily.
   _____

2. Lew is ca rroll wh owro tealic einw ond erlan dw asam athe matic ian.
   _____

3. E.B.Wh iteaut h or ofch arlo tteswe bwa sbo rnin1899.
   _____

4. Han schris tianan ders enwro tefa mousfa iryta lesin clu dingt heu glydu ckling.
   _____

Instructions

Black Out Boxes

Players: One

Materials: Game card, pencil or crayon, atlas, encyclopedias

Goal: Black out boxes to discover a pattern.

Rules:
1. Select a game card from the *Black Out Boxes* series.
2. Read each of the statements on the card. For each true statement black out the box in the square at the bottom of the game card that corresponds to the number of the statement. Black out only the boxes that contain the same number as the true statements.
3. When you have blacked out all the correct boxes, you should see a pattern.
4. Check your answers with the *Black Out Boxes* answer key on the back of the game folder.

Your Animal IQ:

1	2	3	4	5
6	7	8	9	10
11	12	13	14	15
16	17	18	19	20
21	22	23	24	25

These United States:

1	2	3	4	5
6	7	8	9	10
11	12	13	14	15
16	17	18	19	20
21	22	23	24	25

Grasping Graphs:

1	2	3	4	5
6	7	8	9	10
11	12	13	14	15
16	17	18	19	20
21	22	23	24	25

Your Animal IQ

Black out the box in the square below that corresponds to each of the true statements about animals. Use encyclopedias or other reference materials for help.

1. A baby frog looks very much like an adult frog.
2. Flies lay eggs.
3. Whales are mammals.
4. Nymphs (the second stage of grasshopper growth) have no wings.
5. A butterfly is called a larva when it is in its cocoon stage.
6. Marsupials carry their young in pouches.
7. Mother turtles care for their babies for three years before they go into the world alone.
8. The trout is a saltwater fish.
9. Bees make honey using pollen.
10. Leather is made from animal hides.
11. Sea turtles are endangered animals.
12. Most male and female birds of the same species look identical.
13. Frogs are reptiles.
14. Snails do not lay eggs, but rather give birth to live babies.
15. Most sharks have eggs that hatch inside their bodies.
16. The smallest animals alive are made of only one cell.
17. A bald eagle's natural habitat is the rainforest of South America.
18. Cows are carnivorous.
19. Ducks fly north for the winter.
20. Salmon can leap as high as ten feet out of the water.
21. Mother spiders must teach their babies to spin webs because they are not born knowing how.
22. Fish gills help a fish breathe.
23. Wild ducks eat both plants and animals.
24. The dodo bird is extinct.
25. Eagles are herbivores.

1	2	3	4	5
6	7	8	9	10
11	12	13	14	15
16	17	18	19	20
21	22	23	24	25

Name _____ Date _____

Social Studies
Black Out Boxes

These United States

Black out a box in the square below for each of the true statements about states. You may use an atlas or encyclopedias to help you.

1. Texas is the largest state in the United States.
2. Ohio is called the Hoosier State.
3. Atlanta is in Mississippi.
4. Lake Tahoe is on the border of Nevada and Utah.
5. The capital of South Carolina is Richmond.
6. Wyoming seldom gets snow.
7. Baton Rouge is the capital of Louisiana.
8. Estes Park is in Connecticut.
9. The California Redwood is California's state tree.
10. The cardinal is the state bird of Maryland.
11. The city of Billings can be found in Nebraska.
12. Columbus is the capital of Oregon.
13. The roadrunner is New Mexico's state bird.
14. Mount Rushmore is located in Minnesota.
15. The famous Sun Valley Ski Resort is in Colorado.
16. The wild prairie rose is the state flower of North Dakota.
17. Florida is an island.
18. Omaha is the capital of Nebraska.
19. New York is the northernmost state in the United States.
20. Colorado is in the Mountain Time Zone.
21. New Mexico is part of Mexico.
22. Minnesota shares a border with Wisconsin.
23. Interstate 5 runs through California, Oregon, and Washington.
24. To visit the former home of Thomas Jefferson, you would need to go to Virginia.
25. Kansas City is the capital of Kansas.

1	2	3	4	5
6	7	8	9	10
11	12	13	14	15
16	17	18	19	20
21	22	23	24	25

Name_____ Date_____

Black Out Boxes

Grasping Graphs

Refer to the graphs below to decide which of the statements on the next page are true. Black out a square in the box at the bottom of the next page for each true statement.

Statistics from Morgan Elementary School:

Teachers' Favorite Colors

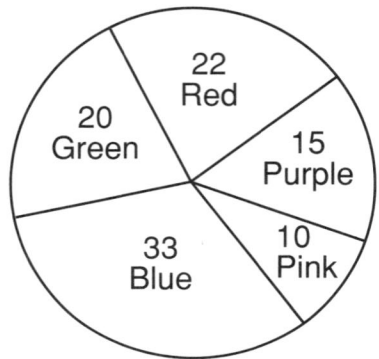

Number of Books Read by Students in Mrs. Neet's Reading Group this Semester

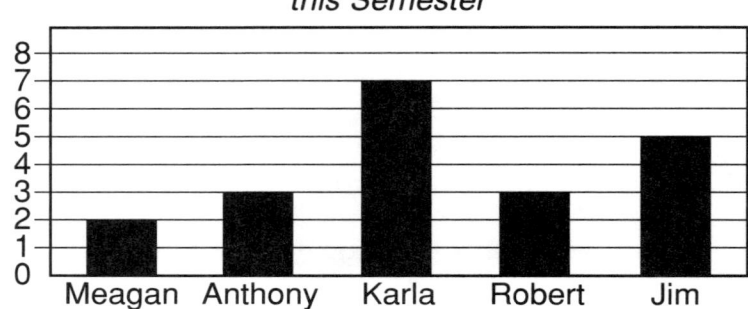

Number of Students Who Dressed in School Colors on Spirit Day

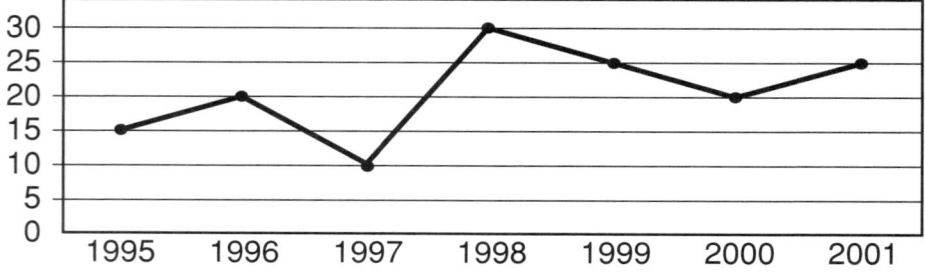

Each 🕺 stands for 6 children

Number of Students in Mrs. Baker's Class

© McGraw-Hill Children's Publishing   IF87061 *Brain Games*

Black Out Boxes
(continued)

1. The favorite color of 33% of the teachers at Morgan Elementary is blue.
2. More sixth graders dressed in school colors on Spirit Day than fourth graders.
3. Karla read 7 books this semester.
4. Mrs. Baker's 2001 class was her largest.
5. Pink is the favorite color of 10% of the teachers at Morgan Elementary.
6. Anthony and Robert each read 3 books this semester.
7. Three third graders dressed for Spirit Day.
8. Meagan is in Mrs. Neet's reading group.
9. In 1995, Mrs. Baker had 25 students in her class.
10. Of the boys in his reading group, Jim has read the most books this semester.
11. Favorite colors of teachers is displayed in a bar graph.
12. More third graders dressed in school colors for Spirit Day than kids in any other grade.
13. More teachers at Morgan Elementary like blue than all the other colors combined.
14. All of the charts and graphs consider statistics from this year only.
15. The number of students in Mrs. Baker's class is displayed on a pie chart.
16. Mrs. Baker has never had more than 35 students in her class.
17. Fewer fourth graders dressed in school colors for Spirit Day than students in any other grade.
18. Together Anthony and Meagan read more books than Robert.
19. Mrs. Baker has the same number of students in her class each year.
20. The Spirit Day graph is a pictograph.
21. The 🧍 symbol equals 6 kids in the Spirit Day graph.
22. Mrs. Baker's class size increases every year.
23. All of the teachers from Morgan Elementary School are represented in the Favorite Colors chart.
24. Eighteen books were read by the students in Mrs. Neet's reading group this semester.
25. Mrs. Baker taught her largest class in 1998.

1	2	3	4	5
6	7	8	9	10
11	12	13	14	15
16	17	18	19	20
21	22	23	24	25

Brain Games
Partner Games

Instructions
You're Out of Order

Players: Two

Materials: Game Card, scissors, reference materials (optional)

Goal: Be the first player to place the events or steps listed on your card in chronological order.

Rules:

1. With your opponent, select one game card from the *You're Out of Order* series.
2. Cut along the bold line in the middle of the game card and give each player half of the page. Each half page lists the same events or steps in identical order.
3. To begin play, each player cuts along the dashed lines between the events or steps on his or her list and then moves the strips of paper around until the player thinks the strips are in chronological or logical order. Players may agree to use or not use encyclopedias, dictionaries, or other reference materials to help them order their paper strips. When a player thinks he or she is finished, that player calls out, "I'm in order!"
4. The player who calls out, "I'm in order!" first checks the answer key to see if the strips are in the correct order. If that player's paper strips are situated in the correct order, then that player is the winner of the game.
5. If the first player to call out, "I'm in order!" has not ordered the events or steps on his or her list correctly, the other player may then attempt to arrange his or her events in the correct order. The answer key is then checked by the second player. If the second player has ordered the events correctly, he or she is the winner of the game.

Answer Key: You're Out of Order

Bug to Butterfly:
1. An adult butterfly lays an egg on a leaf.
2. The egg hatches and a caterpillar emerges.
3. The caterpillar grows because it eats a lot.
4. When it is large enough, the caterpillar stops eating.
5. Now that it is done eating, the caterpillar makes a covering for itself.
6. After it has covered itself in a cocoon, the caterpillar is called a pupa.
7. The pupa undergoes changes inside the cocoon.
8. The changed pupa breaks out of its cocoon as an adult butterfly.

American History:
1. The Boston Tea Party
2. The American Revolution
3. The Civil War
4. The Publication of L. Frank Baum's *The Wonderful Wizard of Oz*
5. Ratification of the 19th Amendment gives women the legal right to vote.
6. Elvis Presley records "Heartbreak Hotel".
7. The Barbie Doll® hits the market.
8. Martin Luther King, Jr. was killed.
9. The Election of George W. Bush

Ordering Equations:
1. .62 x .517 = .32054
2. $\frac{1}{4} + \frac{2}{3} = \frac{11}{12}$
3. .6 + .71 = 1.31
4. Sally got back $3.90 in change.
5. Tom used 6 boxes.
6. Jim ate 9 pieces of pizza.
7. 756 divided by 63 equals 12.
8. The perimeter of a rectangle with the dimension of 12 inches x 23 inches is 276 inches.
9. 324 x 56 = 18,144

Writing a Research Paper:
1. Choose a topic for your research paper.
2. Read about your topic.
3. Take notes on your reading.
4. Using the notes you wrote about what you read, jot down ideas about what information you might include in your first draft.
5. Write a first draft.
6. Have a teacher or fellow student make helpful notes on your first draft.
7. Write a second draft of your paper.
8. Have a friend mark any errors in mechanics and grammar on your second draft.
9. Correct the errors your friend found in your second draft.
10. Write the final draft of your research paper.

Science: You're Out of Order

Bug to Butterfly

The caterpillar grows because it eats a lot.

Now that it is done eating, the caterpillar makes a covering for itself.

The pupa undergoes changes inside the cocoon.

An adult butterfly lays an egg on a leaf.

When it is large enough, the caterpillar stops eating.

After it has covered itself in a cocoon, the caterpillar is called a pupa.

The changed pupa breaks out of its cocoon as an adult butterfly.

The egg hatches and a caterpillar emerges.

- ✂

The caterpillar grows because it eats a lot.

Now that it is done eating, the caterpillar makes a covering for itself.

The pupa undergoes changes inside the cocoon.

An adult butterfly lays an egg on a leaf.

When it is large enough, the caterpillar stops eating.

After it has covered itself in a cocoon, the caterpillar is called a pupa.

The changed pupa breaks out of its cocoon as an adult butterfly.

The egg hatches and a caterpillar emerges.

American History: Then and Now

The American Revolution

The Civil War

The Boston Tea Party

Martin Luther King, Jr. was killed.

The Election of George W. Bush

The Publication of L. Frank Baum's *The Wonderful Wizard of Oz*

Elvis Presley records "Heartbreak Hotel."

The Barbie Doll® hits the market.

Ratification of the 19th Amendment gives women the legal right to vote.

- -

The American Revolution

The Civil War

The Boston Tea Party

Martin Luther King, Jr. was killed.

The Election of George W. Bush

The Publication of L. Frank Baum's *The Wonderful Wizard of Oz*

Elvis Presley records "Heartbreak Hotel."

The Barbie Doll® hits the market.

Ratification of the 19th Amendment gives women the legal right to vote.

Name_____ Date_____

You're Out of Order

Ordering Equations

Solve the math problems and be the first player to order your solutions from least to greatest.

.6 + .71 =

Jim ate three times as many pieces of pizza as Toni at the party. Toni ate 3 pieces. Jim ate _____ pieces of pizza.

Sally bought a $ .45 candy bar and a $ .65 soda with a five-dollar bill. Sally got back $_____ in change.

$\frac{1}{4} + \frac{2}{3} =$

756 divided by 63 equals _____.

The perimeter of a rectangle with the dimension of 12 inches x 23 inches is _____.

324 x 56 =

Tom packed 64 cups into boxes before his move. Each box carried up to 12 cups. Tom used _____ boxes.

.62 x .517 =

- ✂

.6 + .71 =

Jim ate three times as many pieces of pizza as Toni at the party. Toni ate 3 pieces. Jim ate _____ pieces of pizza.

Sally bought a $ .45 candy bar and a $ .65 soda with a five-dollar bill. Sally got back $_____ in charge.

$\frac{1}{4} + \frac{2}{3} =$

756 divided by 63 equals _____.

The perimeter of a rectangle with the dimension of 12 inches x 23 inches is _____.

324 x 56 =

Tom packed 64 cups into boxes before his move. Each box carried up to 12 cups. Tom used _____ boxes.

.62 x .517 =

© McGraw-Hill Children's Publishing   IF87061 *Brain Games*

Language Arts
You're Out of Order

Writing a Research Paper

Write the final draft of your research paper.

Write a first draft.

Take notes on your reading.

Have a teacher or fellow student make helpful notes on your first draft.

Read about your topic.

Correct the errors your friend found in your second draft.

Using the notes you wrote about what you read, jot down ideas about what information you might include in your first draft.

Write a second draft of your paper.

Choose a topic for your research paper.

Have a friend mark any errors in mechanics and grammar on your second draft.

--✂

Write the final draft of your research paper.

Write a first draft.

Take notes on your reading.

Have a teacher or fellow student make helpful notes on your first draft.

Read about your topic.

Correct the errors your friend found in your second draft.

Using the notes you wrote about what you read, jot down ideas about what information you might include in your first draft.

Write a second draft of your paper.

Choose a topic for your research paper.

Have a friend mark any errors in mechanics and grammar on your second draft.

Instructions
Dictionary Detective

Players: Two

Materials: Game cards, scissors, pencils, dictionaries

Goal: Option 1: Be the first player to alphabetize a set of word cards. This option can be played with two to four players.
Option 2: Collect more word cards than your opponent by locating the most words in a dictionary.

Rules: With your opponent, select a game card from the *Dictionary Detective* series.

Option 1:
1. Cut the game card in half. Give each player one-half.
2. Each player cuts apart his or her word cards.
3. Each player arranges his or her word cards in alphabetical order.
4. The first player to finish alphabetizing the words calls out "Dictionary in Order!" The opponent must stop working while the other player checks the answer key.
5. If the player has any cards out of order, he or she must reshuffle all the cards and start again. The opponent may continue ordering his or her cards without shuffling.
6. The first person to arrange his words in alphabetical order correctly is the winner.

See next page for Option 2.

Instructions: Dictionary Detective

Rules:

Option 2:
1. You will need only one set of words. Cut the game card in half and use the top half only.
2. Cut apart the word cards.
3. To begin play, all players choose a word card at the same time. Each player looks up the selected word in a dictionary.
4. When a player locates a word, he or she writes the page number of its location on the word card. Then he or she draws a new card.
5. Play continues until all word cards have been drawn. The player with the most word cards wins.

NOTE: There is no answer key for this game option since page numbers will vary with dictionaries. Check each others' work by swapping cards and verifying that the word on each card can be found on the page recorded.

Answer Key: Dictionary Detective

Science Sayings:
bacteria, biology, diffraction, epidermis, experiment, frequency, fungus, funnel, gravity, illusion, invention, laboratory, machine, magnetism, magnify, optics, oxygen, physics, pressure, reflect

Social Studies Jargon:
amendment, anthropologist, archaeology, battle, biography, colonial, confederation, constitution, continent, controversy, desert, document, equator, geography, longitude, parliament, plateau, political, proclamation, sociology

Math Meanings:
algebra, average, budget, decimal, denominator, dividend, estimate, factor, geometry, graph, multiple, multiply, numerator, parallel, percent, perpendicular, polygon, pyramid, triangle, trigonometry

Writing Words:
author, character, expository, fiction, grammar, imagination, interpretation, language, linguistics, literature, narrative, novel, plot, preposition, pronoun, proofread, speech, story, verbal, vocabulary

Music, Dance, and Drama Words:
allegro, andante, ballet, camera, character, coda, crescendo, fortissimo, improvise, largo, leotard, pointe, position, prelude, role, scene, serenade, stage, tap, tempo

© McGraw-Hill Children's Publishing IF87061 *Brain Games*

Name _____ Date _____

Science Dictionary Detective

Science Sayings

Set One

invention page_____	illusion page_____	biology page_____	physics page_____
bacteria page_____	optics page_____	gravity page_____	machine page_____
reflect page_____	magnify page_____	frequency page_____	epidermis page_____
fungus page_____	diffraction page_____	oxygen page_____	laboratory page_____
experiment page_____	magnetism page_____	funnel page_____	pressure page_____

- ✂

Set Two

invention page_____	illusion page_____	biology page_____	physics page_____
bacteria page_____	optics page_____	gravity page_____	machine page_____
reflect page_____	magnify page_____	frequency page_____	epidermis page_____
fungus page_____	diffraction page_____	oxygen page_____	laboratory page_____
experiment page_____	magnetism page_____	funnel page_____	pressure page_____

© McGraw-Hill Children's Publishing   IF87061 Brain Games

Name _____ **Date** _____

Social Studies Dictionary Detective

Social Studies Jargon

Set One

constitution page_____	geography page_____	political page_____	biography page_____
colonial page_____	parliament page_____	longitude page_____	controversy page_____
continent page_____	sociology page_____	anthropologist page_____	archaeology page_____
proclamation page_____	document page_____	battle page_____	confederation page_____
plateau page_____	amendment page_____	equator page_____	desert page_____

--✂

Set Two

constitution page_____	geography page_____	political page_____	biography page_____
colonial page_____	parliament page_____	longitude page_____	controversy page_____
continent page_____	sociology page_____	anthropologist page_____	archaeology page_____
proclamation page_____	document page_____	battle page_____	confederation page_____
plateau page_____	amendment page_____	equator page_____	desert page_____

Name _____ **Date** _____

Dictionary Detective

Math Meanings

Set One

algebra	geometry	trigonometry	triangle
page____	page____	page____	page____
pyramid	factor	denominator	multiply
page____	page____	page____	page____
decimal	percent	average	budget
page____	page____	page____	page____
estimate	graph	polygon	parallel
page____	page____	page____	page____
numerator	multiple	dividend	perpendicular
page____	page____	page____	page____

Set Two

algebra	geometry	trigonometry	triangle
page____	page____	page____	page____
pyramid	factor	denominator	multiply
page____	page____	page____	page____
decimal	percent	average	budget
page____	page____	page____	page____
estimate	graph	polygon	parallel
page____	page____	page____	page____
numerator	multiple	dividend	perpendicular
page____	page____	page____	page____

© McGraw-Hill Children's Publishing   IF87061 Brain Games

Name _____   **Date** _____

Language Arts
Dictionary Detective

Writing Words

Set One

linguistics page_____	literature page_____	vocabulary page_____	plot page_____
character page_____	fiction page_____	pronoun page_____	preposition page_____
interpretation page_____	language page_____	expository page_____	narrative page_____
imagination page_____	grammar page_____	novel page_____	story page_____
proofread page_____	author page_____	speech page_____	verbal page_____

Set Two

linguistics page_____	literature page_____	vocabulary page_____	plot page_____
character page_____	fiction page_____	pronoun page_____	preposition page_____
interpretation page_____	language page_____	expository page_____	narrative page_____
imagination page_____	grammar page_____	novel page_____	story page_____
proofread page_____	author page_____	speech page_____	verbal page_____

Name _____ Date _____

Performing Arts Dictionary Detective

Music, Dance, and Drama Words

Set One

crescendo page_____	ballet page_____	tap page_____	improvise page_____
role page_____	character page_____	scene page_____	fortissimo page_____
largo page_____	serenade page_____	prelude page_____	andante page_____
allegro page_____	camera page_____	stage page_____	tempo page_____
leotard page_____	pointe page_____	position page_____	coda page_____

------- ✂ -------

Set Two

crescendo page_____	ballet page_____	tap page_____	improvise page_____
role page_____	character page_____	scene page_____	fortissimo page_____
largo page_____	serenade page_____	prelude page_____	andante page_____
allegro page_____	camera page_____	stage page_____	tempo page_____
leotard page_____	pointe page_____	position page_____	coda page_____

Instructions

Drop in the Bucket

Players: Two

Materials: Game cards, scissors

Goal: Be the first player to place the fifteenth-point raindrop on a bucket. Variation: Play with three or four players.

Rules:

1. Each game in this series has two types of cards—bucket cards and raindrop cards. With your opponent, select the game you will play. Make sure you have the correct bucket and raindrop cards for that game.
2. Review the game cards. Printed on each raindrop is a word or phrase and a number of points. A category is listed on each bucket. You and your opponent will be placing raindrops on buckets. A bucket can only hold a raindrop with a word or phrase that fits the category on the bucket.
3. Cut out the buckets and raindrops. Place the buckets faceup on a table. Shuffle the raindrops and deal them evenly between the players.
4. Each player places his or her raindrops facedown in piles that match the categories shown on the buckets. The player also makes a pile for those raindrops that fit into more than one category.
5. The first player chooses a raindrop and places it on the bucket with the matching category. If a raindrop fits more than one category, the player must choose which bucket to use.
6. Play rotates between the players until the points listed on the raindrops in one of the buckets totals exactly 15. The player who placed the last raindrop in that bucket wins the game.
7. If the raindrop points in a bucket exceed 15 points, that bucket can no longer be used to win the game.

Note: If a player places a raindrop in an incorrect bucket, the opponent may claim the misplaced raindrop. Check the answer key if players disagree about where a raindrop may be placed.

Four Sciences:
(Words that fit into more than one category are underlined.)
Astronomy: astronaut, astronomer, stars, asteroids, galaxy, planets, black hole
Technology: Internet, inventions, computers, industrial revolution, cyberspace, fiber optics, electronics
Ecology: <u>rainforest</u>, pollution control, <u>natural resources</u>, conserve, <u>environment</u>, <u>habitat</u>, Earth Day, <u>pandas</u>, <u>animals</u>, <u>plants</u>, <u>mammals</u>, <u>life forms</u>, <u>herbivores</u>
Biology: <u>rainforest</u>, <u>habitat</u>, <u>animals</u>, <u>plants</u>, dissect, <u>herbivores</u>, <u>mammals</u>, <u>life forms</u>, <u>pandas</u>, <u>natural resources</u>, <u>environment</u>

Careers:
(Words that fit into more than one category are underlined.)
Science and Technology Jobs: electrical engineer, medical researcher, anthropologist, <u>surgeon</u>, archaeologist, computer programmer, <u>software salesperson</u>, inventor, <u>sports doctor</u>, <u>physician</u>, <u>nurse</u>
Sports and Entertainment Jobs: baseball player, <u>football coach</u>, <u>sports doctor</u>, singer, actor, dancer, gymnast, <u>voice for commercials</u>
Helping Jobs: <u>sports doctor</u>, <u>physician</u>, teacher, <u>nurse</u>, counselor, <u>surgeon</u>, social worker, tutor, <u>football coach</u>
Sales Jobs: <u>software salesperson</u>, grocery store clerk, real estate agent, advertiser, car salesperson, small business owner, <u>voice for commercials</u>, department store clerk

Magic Multiples:
(Words that fit into more than one category are underlined.)
Multiples of Two: Two, <u>Four</u>, <u>Six</u>, Fourteen, <u>Sixteen</u>, <u>Thirty</u>, <u>Eight</u>, <u>Twelve</u>, <u>Twenty</u>, <u>Forty-four</u>, <u>Four Hundred</u>, <u>Sixty-four</u>, <u>Thirty-six</u>, <u>Forty-eight</u>, <u>Ten</u>, <u>Forty</u>, <u>Fifty</u>, <u>Eighty</u>, <u>One Hundred</u>, <u>Two Thousand</u>, <u>Seventy</u>
Multiples of Three: <u>Six</u>, <u>Thirty</u>, Three, Nine, Twenty-one, Fifteen, Twenty-seven, Thirty-three, Ninety-nine, <u>Twelve</u>, <u>Thirty-six</u>, <u>Forty-eight</u>
Multiples of Four: <u>Four</u>, <u>Sixteen</u>, <u>Eight</u>, <u>Twelve</u>, <u>Twenty</u>, <u>Forty-four</u>, <u>Four Hundred</u>, <u>Sixty-four</u>, <u>Thirty-six</u>, <u>Forty-eight</u>, <u>Forty</u>, <u>Eighty</u>, <u>One Hundred</u>, <u>Two Thousand</u>
Multiples of Ten: <u>Thirty</u>, <u>Twenty</u>, <u>Four Hundred</u>, <u>Ten</u>, <u>Forty</u>, <u>Fifty</u>, <u>Eighty</u>, <u>One Hundred</u>, <u>Two Thousand</u>, <u>Seventy</u>

Parts of Speech:
(Words that fit into more than one category are underlined.)
Nouns: dog, car, <u>love</u>, Mr. Jones, Dallas, Utah, hat
Verbs: thinks, sat, sings, stop, run, drove, was, <u>love</u>
Adverbs: quickly, slowly, swiftly, exactly, angrily, correctly, nicely
Adjectives: blue, fast, large, nice, pretty, shiny, silly

Four Arts:
(Words that fit into more than one category are underlined.)
Photography: film, camera, photograph, <u>visual art</u>, <u>black and white</u>, <u>portrait</u>, flash
Sketching: <u>canvas</u>, <u>visual art</u>, <u>black and white</u>, <u>portrait</u>, pencils, charcoal, eraser, draw, drawing, <u>shading</u>, doodle, <u>pastels</u>
Painting: <u>canvas</u>, <u>visual art</u>, <u>portrait</u>, <u>shading</u>, paint, paintbrush, oils, <u>pastels</u>, palette, color wheel, <u>black and white</u>
Sculpting: <u>visual art</u>, <u>portrait</u>, clay, stone, marble, wood, carve, mold, ice

Name _____ **Date** _____

Drop in the Bucket
(Game Card A)

Four Sciences

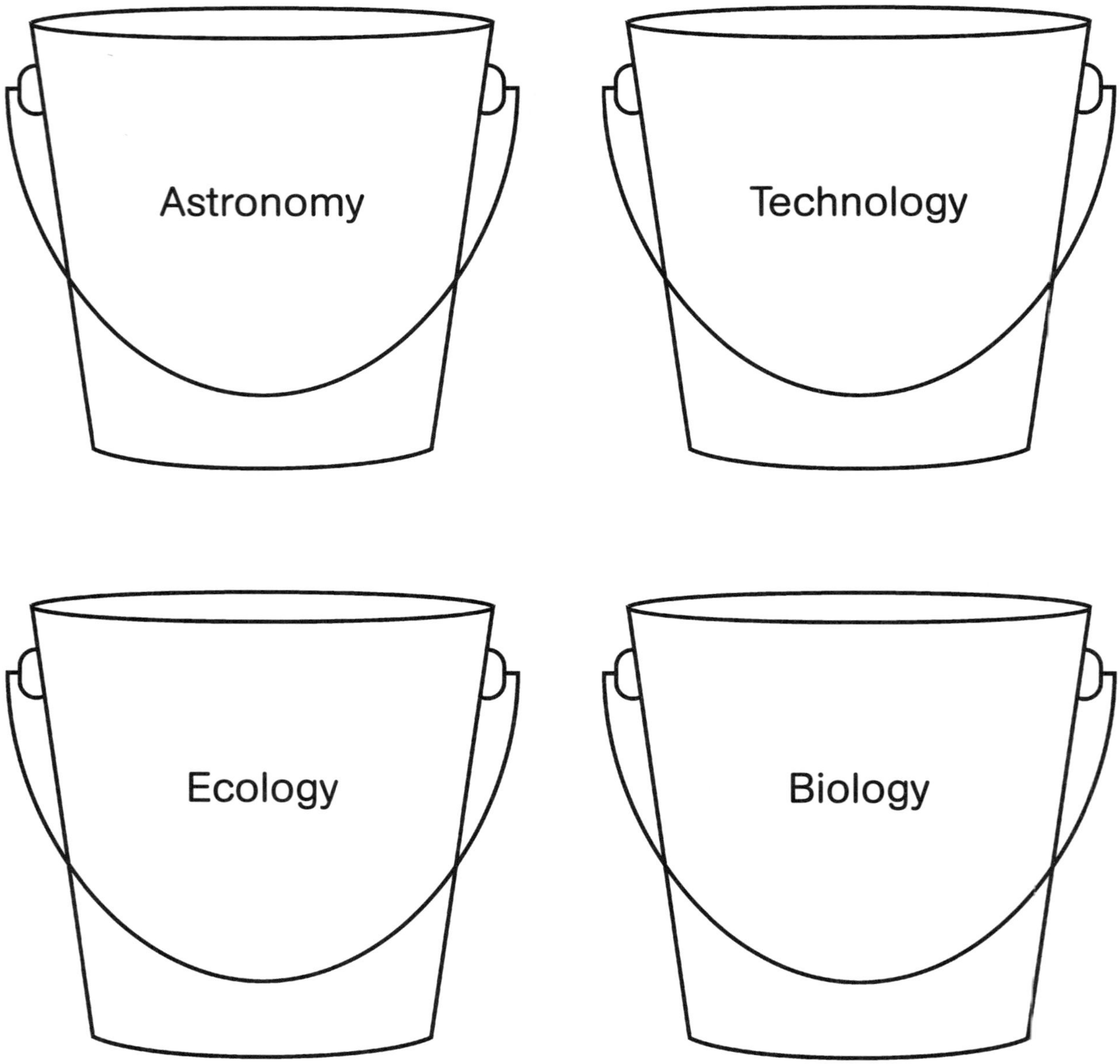

- Astronomy
- Technology
- Ecology
- Biology

© McGraw-Hill Children's Publishing

IF87061 *Brain Games*

Name _____ **Date** _____

Science
Drop in the Bucket
(Game Card B)

Four Sciences

5 points ASTRONAUT	5 points INTERNET	5 points CONSERVE	5 points ANIMALS
4 points ASTRONOMER	4 points INVENTIONS	4 points RAINFOREST	4 points PLANTS
3 points STARS	3 points COMPUTERS	3 points POLLUTION CONTROL	3 points DISSECT
2 points ASTEROIDS	2 points GALAXY	2 points INDUSTRIAL REVOLUTION	2 points CYBERSPACE
2 points NATURAL RESOURCES	2 points PANDAS	2 points MAMMALS	2 points ENVIRONMENT
1 point PLANETS	1 point BLACK HOLE	1 point FIBER OPTICS	1 point ELECTRONICS
1 point HABITAT	1 point EARTH DAY	1 point HERBIVORES	1 point LIFE FORMS

© McGraw-Hill Children's Publishing   IF87061 *Brain Games*

Name _____   Date _____

Social Studies
Drop in the Bucket
(Game Card A)

Careers

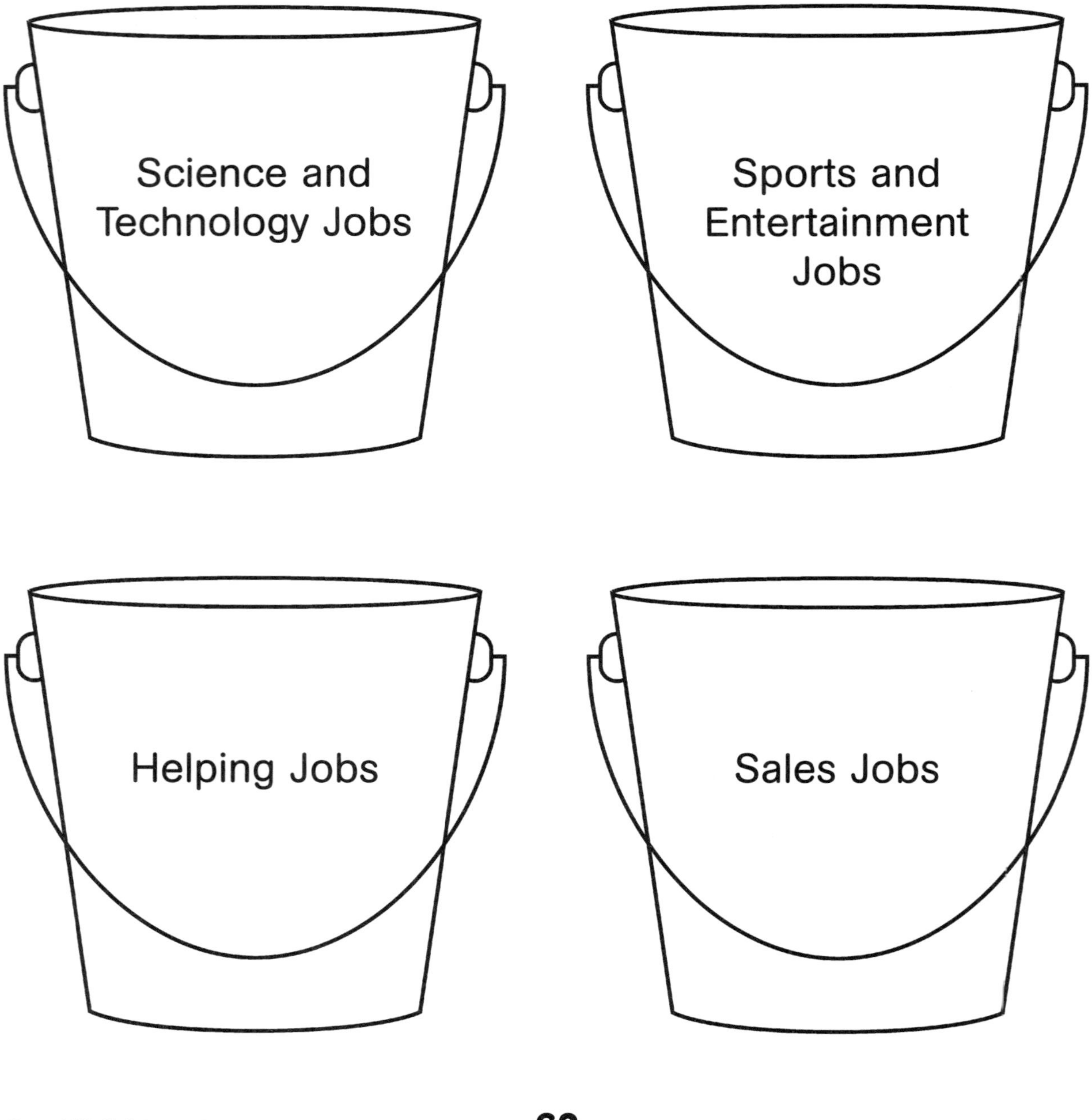

- Science and Technology Jobs
- Sports and Entertainment Jobs
- Helping Jobs
- Sales Jobs

Magic Multiples

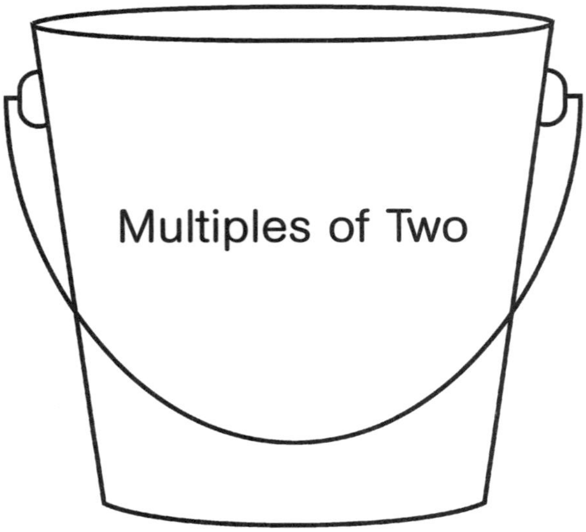

Multiples of Two

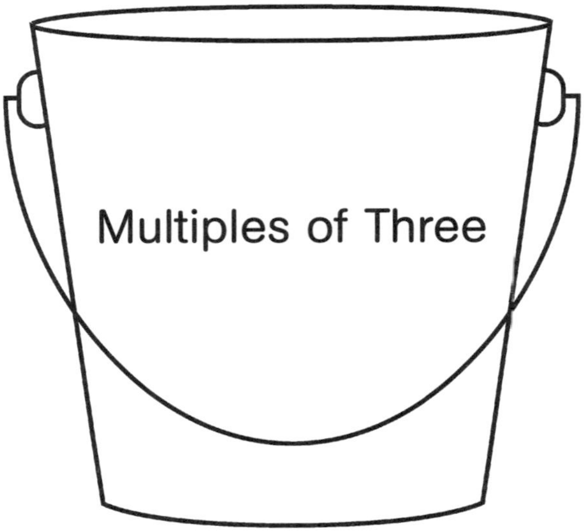

Multiples of Three

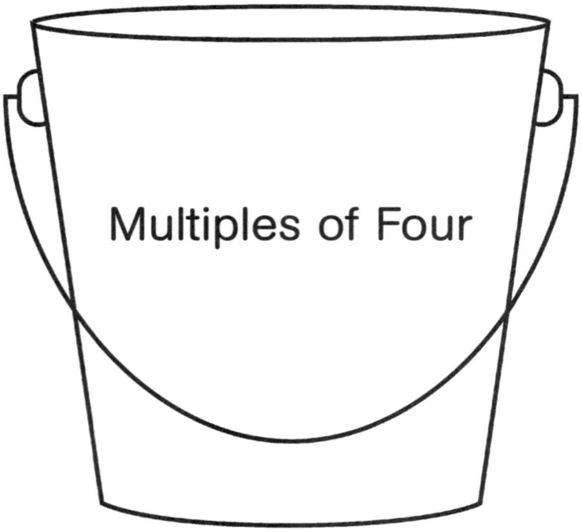

Multiples of Four

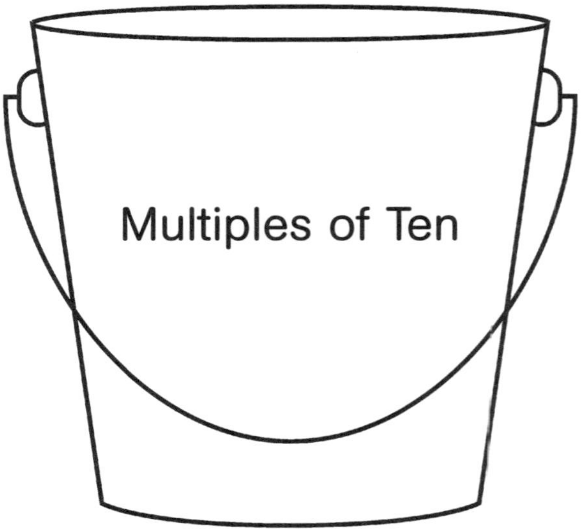

Multiples of Ten

Name _____ Date _____

Drop in the Bucket
(Game Card A)

Parts of Speech

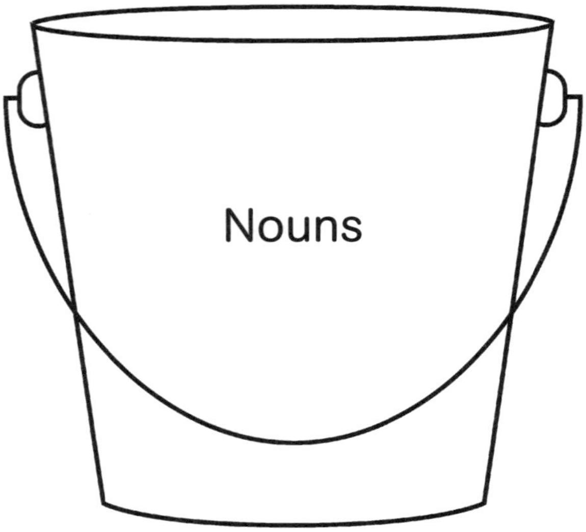

Nouns

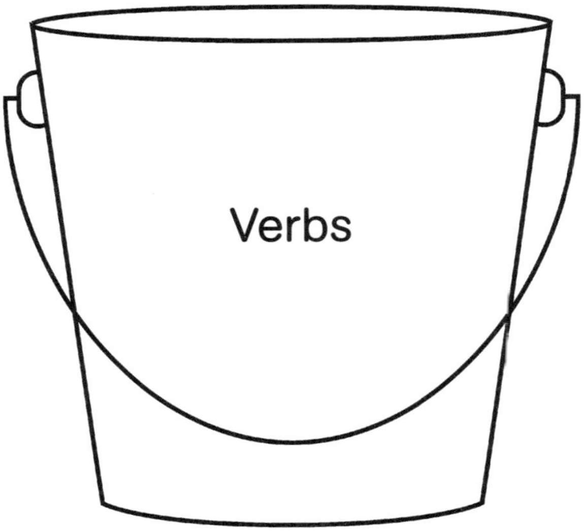

Verbs

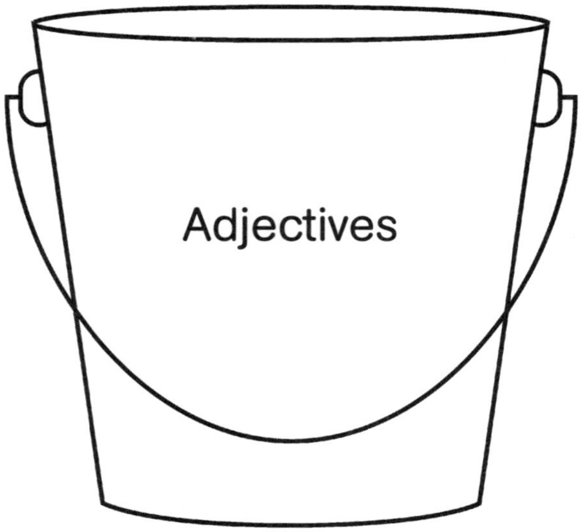

Adjectives

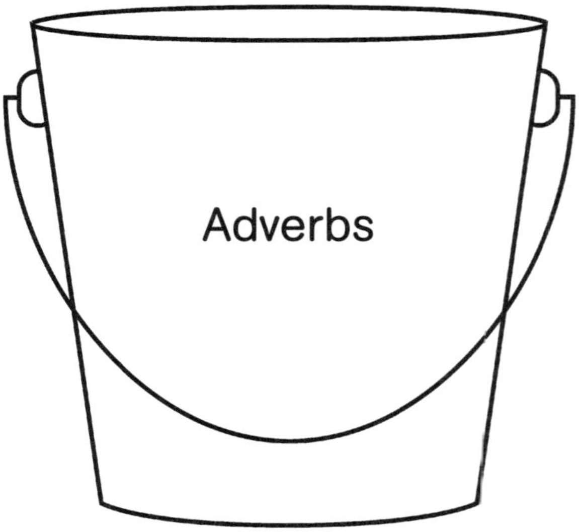

Adverbs

Name _____ Date _____

Art
Drop in the Bucket
(Game Card A)

Four Arts

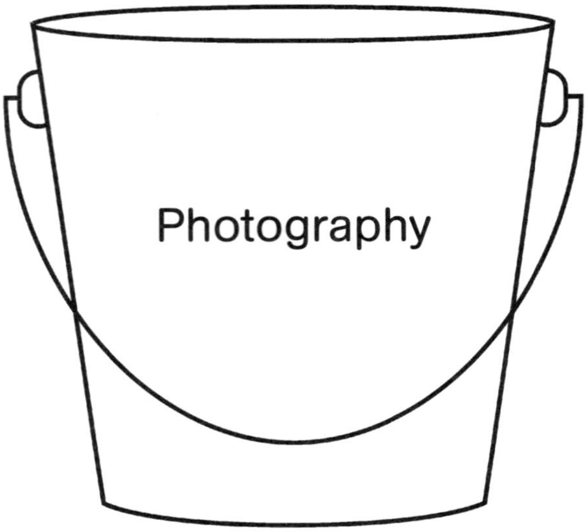

Photography

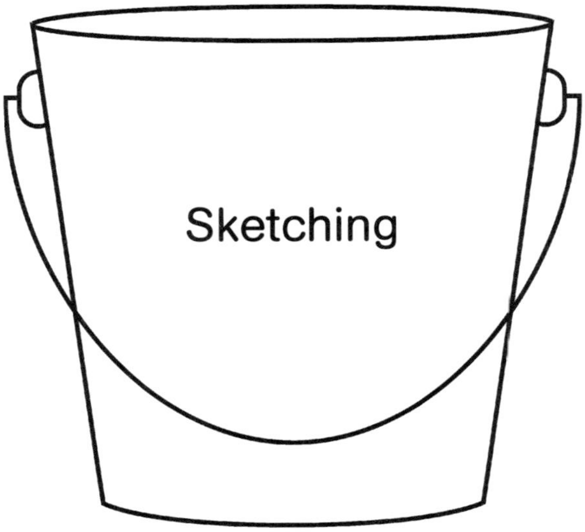

Sketching

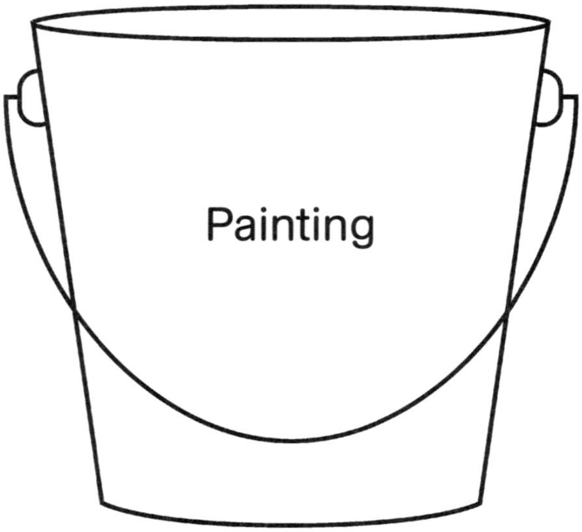

Painting

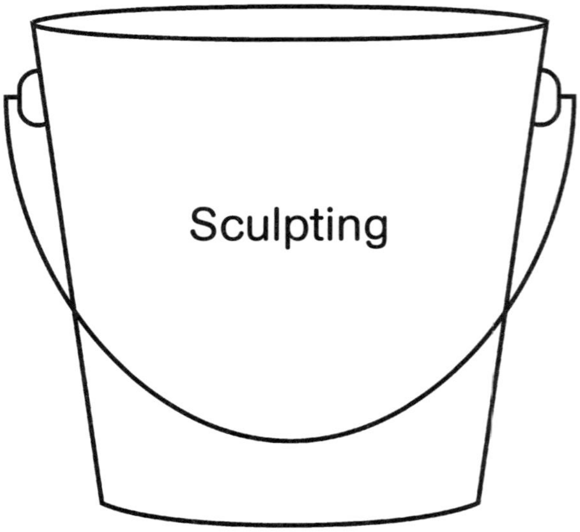

Sculpting

© McGraw-Hill Children's Publishing **68** IF87061 *Brain Games*

Name _____ **Date** _____

Art
Drop in the Bucket
(Game Card B)

Four Arts

5 points FILM	5 points CANVAS	5 points VISUAL ART	5 points CLAY
4 points CAMERA	4 points PENCILS	4 points SHADING	4 points STONE
3 points CHARCOAL	3 points PAINT	3 points MARBLE	3 points PHOTOGRAPH
2 points BLACK AND WHITE	2 points ERASER	2 points PAINTBRUSH	2 points WOOD
2 points PORTRAIT	2 points DRAW	2 points OILS	2 points CARVE
1 point DRAWING	1 point FLASH	1 point DOODLE	1 point PASTELS
1 point PALETTE	1 point COLOR WHEEL	1 point MOLD	1 point ICE

© McGraw-Hill Children's Publishing   IF87061 *Brain Games*

Instructions: Look It Up

Players: Two

Materials: Game cards, pencil, encyclopedias
Variation: Play with three or four players

Goal: Collect more cards than your opponent by using encyclopedias to answer questions.

Rules:

1. Select a game card from the *Look It Up* series. Cut along the black lines to create 20 individual cards.
2. Place the cards facedown on a table or desk between the two players.
3. Both players select a card at the same time. Players read their cards and use an encyclopedia to help fill in the blank or answer the question written there. When a player finds the answer to the question, he or she writes it on the card and keeps the card. That player then selects a new card and locates the answer to that question. Play continues until all cards have been collected.
4. Check your answers with the *Look It Up* answer key on the back of the game folder. The student who answers the most questions correctly wins the game.

Notes: 1. If a needed encyclopedia is not available because your opponent is using it, you may turn your card back over to its original position on the table and choose another one.
2. If you cannot locate the answer to a question on a card, you may return it to the table and choose another card. Keep in mind that your opponent may find the answer that you did not find.

Answer Key
Look It Up

Inventions and Discoveries:
- A. Eli Whitney
- B. peanut
- C. Alexander Fleming
- D. 1822
- E. Cornelius Drebbell
- F. 1908
- G. Nicolas Appert
- H. Wright
- I. Marie
- J. Alexander Graham Bell
- K. evolution
- L. 32
- M. 1706
- N. 1931
- O. New Jersey
- P. 1896
- Q. Jacob Fussel
- R. England, or 1791
- S. relativity
- T. psychology

Dates and Places in History:
- A. Babylon
- B. 3000 B.C.
- C. 1350 to 1650
- D. Fifth
- E. 1941
- F. Europe
- G. 1846
- H. 1854
- I. 1789 to 1797
- J. Ireland
- K. Dec. 16, 1773
- L. 1509–1547
- M. Oct. 16, 1962
- N. 4
- O. New York
- P. The United States of America
- Q. 17th
- R. 1948
- S. I
- T. North America

Number Names:
- A. calculus
- B. around 582 B.C.
- C. Greece
- D. three
- E. triangles
- F. parallel
- G. Sicily
- H. England
- I. University of Cambridge
- J. Germany
- K. 1564
- L. France
- M. 16
- N. Blaise Pascal
- O. computers
- P. Germany
- Q. Mathematical Treatise in Nine Sections
- R. China
- S. Leonardo of Pisa
- T. Scotland

Trivial Tidbits:
- A. Southwest State Teacher's College
- B. horse and donkey
- C. Dennis the Menace
- D. hair
- E. 35
- F. The Amazon
- G. Ch'ing
- H. 1912
- I. high
- J. Abyssinia
- K. *Gone with the Wind*
- L. 4
- M. no
- N. Michelangelo
- O. Latin
- P. Colorado
- Q. New Zealand
- R. Crimean
- S. first American in space
- T. first African American congresswoman

Name _____ Date _____

Inventions and Discoveries

A. Who invented the cotton gin? _____	B. George Washington Carver found hundreds of uses for the sweet potato and the _____.	C. Penicillin was discovered by _____.	D. Louis Pasteur, the inventor of pasteurization, was born in _____.
E. The submarine was built in 1620 by _____ _____.	F. Cellophane was invented in _____ by Jacques Brandenberger.	G. The process of canning was invented by the French chef, _____ _____.	H. The _____ brothers experimented with airplanes.
I. _____ Curie and her husband Pierre experimented with radioactivity.	J. The telephone was invented by _____ _____.	K. Charles Darwin proposed the theory of _____.	L. Gabriel Fahrenheit devised a temperature scale in which water freezes at _____ degrees.
M. The American scientist Ben Franklin was born in _____.	N. Thomas Edison died in _____.	O. Thomas Edison's research lab was in the state of _____.	P. Henry Ford produced his first automobile in the year _____.
Q. The first commercial maker of ice cream in America was _____.	R. The inventor Michael Faraday was born in _____.	S. Albert Einstein suggested the theory of _____.	T. Sigmund Freud was a pioneer in the science of _____.

© McGraw-Hill Children's Publishing   IF87061 *Brain Games*

Name_____ Date_____

Dates and Places in History

A. Hammurabi's Code lists the laws of what ancient land? _____	B. Egyptian hieroglyphics were first used around what century? _____	C. The Renaissance era in Europe existed from about _____ to _____.	D. The Middle Ages refers to a period of time beginning in the _____ century.
E. The United States entered World War II in _____.	F. World War I was fought on which continent? _____	G. Iowa became a state in what year? _____	H. In what year was the Kansas-Nebraska Act enacted by Congress? _____
I. George Washington was President of the United States from _____ to _____.	J. The Potato Famine struck what country in 1845? _____	K. On what date did the Boston Tea Party take place? _____	L. When did Henry VIII reign in Britain? _____
M. The Cuban Missile Crisis officially began on what date? _____	N. How many times was Franklin Roosevelt elected to the presidency? _____	O. James DeLancey was Supreme Court Justice of what state in 1733? _____	P. The Mexican War began in 1846 when what country annexed Texas? _____
Q. Andrew Johnson was the _____ President of the United States.	R. India became an independent nation in what year? _____	S. Which Napoleon was the famous general (I, II, or III)? _____	T. The French and Indian Wars took place on what continent? _____

© McGraw-Hill Children's Publishing   IF87061 Brain Games

Number Names

A. Isaac Newton invented a branch of math called _____.	B. Pythagorean's theorem was written by a man born in what year? _____	C. The mathematician named Euclid lived here. _____	D. Solid geometry deals with _____-dimensional shapes.
E. Trigonometry is a branch of math that studies what shape? _____	F. The bases of a prism are two _____ planes.	G. Where was Archimedes born? _____	H. Bertrand Russell was a mathematician from _____.
I. Alfred Whitehead taught math at what college from 1885–1911? _____ _____	J. Albert Einstein was born in what country? _____.	K. In what year was Galileo born? _____	L. Blaise Pascal was born in what country? _____
M. Blaise Pascal wrote a math theorem at the age of _____.	N. Who invented the adding machine in 1642? _____	O. Charles Babbage built machines that gave rise to _____.	P. Georg Cantor was a mathematician from _____.
Q. Qin Jinshao wrote a book called _____ _____ _____.	R. Zhu Shijie was an ancient mathematician from _____.	S. Leonardo Fibonacci is also known as _____	T. John Napier was a mathematician from _____.

Name_____ Date_____

Trivia: Look It Up

Trivial Tidbits

A. President Lyndon B. Johnson graduated from this college in 1930. _____	B. A mule is a cross between what two animals? _____	C. Hank Ketcham created what famous cartoon? _____	D. What is a rhino's horn made of? _____
E. How many eyes does a scallop have? _____	F. What is the longest river in South America? _____	G. What was the name of China's last imperial dynasty? _____	H. In what year did Jim Thorpe win Olympic medals? _____
I. Yaks live at high or low altitudes? _____	J. What was the former name of Ethiopia? _____	K. Margaret Mitchell wrote what book? _____	L. How many of the Great Lakes border Canada? _____
M. Was the Underground Railroad a railroad? _____	N. Who painted the Sistine Chapel? _____	O. Romance languages are derived from what language? _____	P. The Hoover Dam is located on what river? _____
Q. What country owns the Auckland Islands? _____	R. Florence Nightingale cared for soldiers during this war. _____	S. What was Alan B. Shepard Jr.'s claim to fame? _____	T. What is Shirley Chisholm's claim to fame? _____

© McGraw-Hill Children's Publishing   75   IF87061 Brain Games

Instructions

Four-Minute Fury

Players: Two

Materials: Game cards, pencil, timer or watch alarm, reference materials such as encyclopedias, atlases, and textbooks

Goal: Answer the most questions correctly in four minutes.

Rules:

1. With your opponent, select a game card from the *Four-Minute Fury* series. Cut the game card in half and give one-half to each player. The bottom and top halves of each card are identical.
2. Decide whether or not you will use reference materials.
3. Set a timer or watch alarm for four minutes.
4. Each player answers as many questions as possible in four minutes.
5. When the alarm or timer rings, players put down pencils and check their answers in the *Four-Minute Fury* answer key on the back of the game folder. The player who answers the most questions correctly is the winner.

Answer Key
Four-Minute Fury

Science Fury:
1. water droplets
2. a very low cloud
3. water in the form of gas
4. solid, liquid, gas
5. hydrogen and oxygen
6. the process of water vapor turning into liquid water
7. the process of liquid water turning into water vapor
8. warm air
9. the fastest part of a stream
10. a man-made lake where drinking water is stored
11. metamorphic, sedimentary, igneous
12. two of these: rain, ice, wind, sun, plants

Geographic Fury:
1. a level area atop a mountain
2. a body of land completely surrounded by water
3. an inlet of the ocean parallel to the coast
4. a body of land surrounded by water on three sides
5. a narrow body of water connecting two larger bodies of water
6. a dry area
7. a point of land that extends into water
8. altitude
9. an imaginary circle around the middle of the earth
10. a chain of rocks lying in or near water
11. a triangle of land deposit at the mouth of a river
12. a narrow strip of land connecting two larger land areas.

Math Fury Row One:

A. 57	6	988	66	135	4	177	228
B. 49	31	131	7	207	389	4	103
C. 1131	448	156	31	472	66	39	108
D. 131	49	390	8	6	703	608	43

Literacy Fury:
1. a figure of speech in which a comparison is implied by analogy but is not stated
2. a comparison of two things that are unlike, usually using the words *like* or *as*
3. an expression that does not mean what it literally says
4. a word, phrase, or number with the same sequence of letters or numbers whether read from right to left or left to right
5. an apparently contradictory statement that suggests a truth
6. a general comparability or likeness
7. a work, often humorous, that imitates another, usually serious, work
8. a story of heroic deeds and events
9. a conversation between two or more people
10. a stanza of five lines with a specific number of syllables used in each line
11. a type of poem written in three lines with a specific number of syllables used in each line
12. the use of words the sound of which suggests their meanings

Name _____ Date _____

Science: Four-Minute Fury

Science Fury

Answer as many questions as you can in four minutes.

1. What is a cloud made of? _____
2. What is fog? _____
3. What is water vapor? _____
4. What are the three forms water can take? _____
5. Of what atoms is a water molecule made? _____
6. What is condensation? _____
7. What is evaporation? _____
8. Which is lighter—warm air or cold water? _____
9. What is a water current? _____
10. What is a reservoir? _____
11. Name the three main kinds of rocks: _____
12. Name at least two things that break down rocks into smaller rocks. _____

--✂

Answer as many questions as you can in four minutes.

1. What is a cloud made of? _____
2. What is fog? _____
3. What is water vapor? _____
4. What are the three forms water can take? _____
5. Of what atoms is a water molecule made? _____
6. What is condensation? _____
7. What is evaporation? _____
8. Which is lighter—warm air or cold water? _____
9. What is a water current? _____
10. What is a reservoir? _____
11. Name the three main kinds of rocks: _____
12. Name at least two things that break down rocks into smaller rocks. _____

© McGraw-Hill Children's Publishing   IF87061 *Brain Games*

Name _____ Date _____

Social Studies: Four-Minute Fury

Geography Fury
Define as many geography terms as you can in four minutes.

1. plateau _____
2. island _____
3. sound _____
4. peninsula _____
5. strait _____
6. desert _____
7. cape _____
8. elevation _____
9. equator _____
10. reef _____
11. delta _____
12. isthmus _____

--✂

Define as many geography terms as you can in four minutes.

1. plateau _____
2. island _____
3. sound _____
4. peninsula _____
5. strait _____
6. desert _____
7. cape _____
8. elevation _____
9. equator _____
10. reef _____
11. delta _____
12. isthmus _____

Four-Minute Fury

Math Fury
Solve as many problems as possible in four minutes. Watch for sign changes!

A. 12 +45	34 −28	76 x13	37 +29	88 +47	92 −88	129 +48	76 x 3
B. 95 −46	4)124	86 +45	45 −38	23 x 9	988 −599	9)36	96 + 7
C. 87 x13	56 x 8	67 +89	98 −67	59 x 8	232 −166	2)78	63 +45
D. 99 + 32	34 +15	78 x 5	96 −88	83 −77	235 +468	76 x 8	88 −45

--- ✂

Solve as many problems as possible in four minutes. Watch for sign changes!

A. 12 +45	34 −28	76 x13	37 +29	88 +47	92 −88	129 +48	76 x 3
B. 95 −46	4)124	86 +45	45 −38	23 x 9	988 −599	9)36	96 + 7
C. 87 x13	56 x 8	67 +89	98 −67	59 x 8	232 −166	2)78	63 +45
D. 99 + 32	34 +15	78 x 5	96 −88	83 −77	235 +468	76 x 8	88 −45

Name _____ Date _____

Language Arts
Four-Minute Fury

Literacy Fury

Define as many literacy terms as you can in four minutes.

1. metaphor _____
2. simile _____
3. idiom _____
4. palindrome _____
5. paradox _____
6. analogy _____
7. parody _____
8. saga _____
9. dialogue _____
10. cinquain _____
11. haiku _____
12. onomatopoeia _____

Define as many literacy terms as you can in four minutes.

1. metaphor _____
2. simile _____
3. idiom _____
4. palindrome _____
5. paradox _____
6. analogy _____
7. parody _____
8. saga _____
9. dialogue _____
10. cinquain _____
11. haiku _____
12. onomatopoeia _____

Instructions

Matching Madness

Players: Two

Materials: Game cards, scissors

Goal: Locate the most matching cards.
Variation: Play with three or four players

Rules:
1. Select a game card from the *Matching Madness* series. Cut along the black lines to create twenty individual cards.
2. Shuffle the cards. Arrange them facedown on a table or desk in five rows of four.
3. Decide who will begin play. Player One turns over two cards. If the cards turned over match according to category, Player One takes the cards. If they do not match, Player One returns the cards to their original position on the table or desk.
4. Play continues with Player Two turning over two cards. When all cards have been collected, players count their cards. The player with the most cards wins.

Same Science:
Rock types—sandstone, marble; Cloud types—cumulus, cirrus; Flowers—tulip, rose; Trees—oak, pine; Mammals—dolphin, bear; Insects—fly, beetle; Amphibians—frog, salamander; Reptiles—lizard, snake; Natural disasters—tornado, hurricane; Simple machines—lever, pulley

Capital Connection:
Frankfort, Kentucky; Boston, Massachusetts; Helena, Montana; Lincoln, Nebraska; Trenton, New Jersey; Harrisburg, Pennsylvania; Montpelier, Vermont; Olympia, Washington; Charleston, West Virginia; Albany, New York

Divide and Conquer:
$16 \div 4 = 4$; $32 \div 4 = 8$; $72 \div 8 = 9$; $35 \div 7 = 5$; $48 \div 8 = 6$; $49 - 7 = 7$; $18 \div 6 = 3$; $100 \div 10 = 10$; $40 \div 20 = 2$; $44 \div 4 = 11$

Abbr. for Short:
M.D.—Medical Doctor; Mr.—Mister; No.—Number; St.—Saint; Jr.—Junior; Ave.—Avenue; U.S.A.—United States of America; FBI—Federal Bureau of Investigation; Co.—Company; Inc.—Incorporated

Name_____ Date_____

Same Science

Find the two words in each of the following categories: rock types, cloud types, flowers, trees, mammals, insects, amphibians, reptiles, natural disasters, simple machines.

SANDSTONE	TORNADO	FLY	CUMULUS
CIRRUS	MARBLE	DOLPHIN	SNAKE
LIZARD	OAK	BEAR	TULIP
FROG	PULLEY	BEETLE	SALAMANDER
PINE	LEVER	HURRICANE	ROSE

Name_____   Date _____

Capital Connection

Match the states with their capitals.

KENTUCKY	NEW JERSEY	NEW YORK	WASHINGTON
OLYMPIA	CHARLESTON	PENNSYLVANIA	BOSTON
MASSACHUSETTS	FRANKFORT	LINCOLN	WEST VIRGINIA
HELENA	MONTPELIER	HARRISBURG	MONTANA
NEBRASKA	TRENTON	VERMONT	ALBANY

© McGraw-Hill Children's Publishing   IF87061 Brain Games

Divide and Conquer

Match the division equations with their solutions.

16 ÷ 4	100 ÷ 10	11	7
4	32 ÷ 4	44 ÷ 4	6
8	72 ÷ 8	48 ÷ 8	5
9	35 ÷ 7	49 ÷ 7	40 ÷ 20
18 ÷ 6	3	10	2

Abbr. for Short

Match the words with their abbreviations.

M.D.	U.S.A.	Federal Bureau of Investigation	Co.
Medical Doctor	Incorporated	United States of America	Ave.
Avenue	Company	Mr.	Saint
No.	Mister	FBI	Inc.
Number	St.	Jr.	Junior

Brain Games

Games for the Entire Class

Instructions: Five Minutes Flat

Players: Entire class

Materials: Game cards, common classroom items used as props

Goal: Create and act out a scene using props, poses, character descriptions, and dialogue lines in five minutes or less.

Rules:

1. Divide the class into groups of three or four. Number your groups.
2. Copy all game cards from the *Five Minutes Flat* series. Cut along the dotted lines to create ten individual scenes. Distribute one scene card to Group One.
3. Group One has five minutes to create a scene using the props and characters given. The characters must either begin or end the scene in the poses given, and one of the characters must speak the given line at some point during the scene.
4. Following five minutes of preparation, challenge Group One to present their scene, which should last no longer than five minutes.
5. Distribute a scene card to Group Two. Continue play until all groups have had a chance to present a scene.

To be read by the teacher to students:
1. If your group has three people, cut one of the characters described on your card from the scene before you begin.
2. Since you have only five minutes to prepare your scene, do not spend time writing a detailed script. Just agree upon a general story line and then improvise your lines as you go. Remember, however, one character must say the given line at some point during your scene.
3. This is not a competitive game. You will not be judged against other groups. There is no right way to act out your scene. Just make it up and have fun!

SCI FI Scenes

The Time Machine

Props: One student desk or table, a marker, five sheets of paper

Characters:
Kevin and Jeffrey—modern-day high school football players
Sarah—Kevin and Jeffrey's friend
Bud—a teenage cowboy out of the 1800's

Poses:
Kevin is posed ready to throw a football.
Jeffrey looks ready to catch Kevin's throw.
Sarah watches Kevin and Jeffrey with her hands on her hips.
Bud looking at Sarah with wide eyes.

Line: Well, I'm going with him!

Oblee the Alien

Props: One student desk or table, a stapler, a roll of tape

Characters:
Oblee—a shy, female alien
Professor Smart—an old, clumsy college science professor
Dean—a tough-guy student of Professor Smart's
Meagan—Dean's little sister

Poses:
Oblee crouches under the desk with hands over ears.
Professor Smart sits on the floor with one hand to his forehead.
Dean stands with his mouth open wide and his arms in the air.
Meagan leans over in front of Oblee with her back to the audience.

Line: I have no clue!

Name _____ Date _____

Social Studies
Five Minutes Flat

Culture Clash Scenes

Only in America

Props: flag, pencil, pad of paper

Characters:
Abraham Lincoln
Elvis
Uncle Sam
Jim Carey

Poses:
Abraham Lincoln is posed as though giving a speech.
Elvis sings into a microphone.
Uncle Sam stands tall, straight, in a pose of singing opera.
Jim Carey sports a wide-mouthed laugh.

Line: One at a time. One at a time!

Linda Gets a Taste of Her Own Medicine

Props: a bowl or coffee cup, pencil

Characters:
Tika—a new student from Thailand
Mrs. Carper—Tika's home economics teacher
Linda—An excellent cook but a very conceited student
Mindy—Tika's cooking partner

Poses:
Tika makes a face as though she has just tasted something awful.
Mrs. Carper looks at Linda and grins widely.
Linda stands with hands on hips looking at Tika in disbelief and anger.
Mindy laughs and looks at Linda.

Line: I guess I don't understand your way of cooking.

Making Money Scenes

I Quit!

Props: two textbooks, a newspaper, a desk

Characters:
Rick—a clumsy preteen who is eager to earn money
Mr. Barker—a newspaper editor
Mrs. Kennedy—a bookstore owner
Mom—Rick's mom

Poses:
Rick stands with his hands in the air.
Mr. Baker stands with his hands in the air.
Mrs. Kennedy stands with her hands in the air.
Mom stands with her hands crossed over her chest.

Line: I give up!

The Bet

Props: a table, three chairs

Characters:
Cindy, Karen, Ashley, Jeff—four middle school friends in competition on a fund-raising drive

Poses:
The girls are seated in chairs behind the table, facing the audience.
Cindy has her elbows on the table and her head in her hands.
Karen is in a pose of speaking.
Ashley is looking at Karen.
Jeff is standing off to one side of the table.

Line: The whole thing was a bad idea anyway.

Readers and Writers Scenes

Career Day Surprise

Props: a book, a desk, a chair

Characters:
Mrs. Sills—a middle school teacher
Stacy and Liz—students in Mrs. Sill's class
Mr. Henderson—a visiting author on Career Day in Mrs. Sill's class

Poses:
Stacy and Mr. Henderson are shaking hands.
Mrs. Sills is smiling.
Liz is rolling her eyes.

Line: I can't believe we're shaking hands!

Nervous No More

Props: four papers, three chairs and desks

Characters:
Nick—a student who writes well but hates to speak in front of the class
Bill—a class clown who seldom completes his homework
Ryan—Nick's friend
Lindsay—another student who writes well but hates to speak in front of the class

Poses:
A paper held in Nick's hand shakes as he gives a speech to his class.
Bill is seated and laughing, looking at Nick.
Ryan is looking over Bill's shoulder at his paper.
Lindsay is sitting still, watching Nick speak.

Line: There isn't a single word written on his paper!

Name _____ Date _____

Performing Arts
Five Minutes Flat

Singing Fool Scenes

Opening Night

Props: four pieces of paper

Characters:
Sam, Deidra, Leann, Jarad—students in a school choir

Poses:
All characters stand holding their papers with their mouths open in a pose of singing.

Line: I can't believe we pulled it off!

-- ✂

The Show Must Go On

Props: two pencils, a desk, a chair

Characters:
Kerry—a teenage guitar player who is leader of a rock band which plays weekend gigs
Ted—the band's singer
Melissa—the band's drummer
Eddy—the band's teenage manager

Poses:
Kerry looks toward Eddy.
Ted holds his throat with a pained look on his face.
Melissa sits on chair and drums the desk with the two pencils.
Eddy's hands are outstretched to Kerry, mouth open in a pose of shouting.

Line: I don't care if Ted is on his deathbed, you are not singing lead on Saturday night!

Instructions

Speak Your Mind

Players: Entire class

Materials: Game cards, scissors

Object: Students practice public speaking skills as they talk at random about given subjects.

Rules:
1. Select a game card from the *Speak Your Mind* series.
2. Cut the cards along the black lines to create individual word or phrase cards.
3. Shuffle the cards and place them facedown in a single stack.
4. Select a student to begin play. Player One selects the first card from the stack. That person has one minute to think about the topic listed on the card. The student then speaks about the topic for two minutes. In the event that a student chooses a topic about which he or she knows absolutely nothing, another topic may be chosen.
5. The student's information about the topic may include real or fabricated stories, examples, explanations, justifications, descriptions, details, opinions, or any other information. Talk may be random phrases related to the topic, thought-out sentences and ideas related to the topic, or fully-developed stories. The idea of the game is to give each student a chance to talk in front of other members of the class. Students do not need to worry about making sense, but only about sticking to the topic and talking for two minutes.
6. Continue play until all players have had a turn to talk about one topic. Topics may be used more than once if there are more than twenty students in the class.

Name_____ Date_____

Speak Your Mind

Talk About Science

Talk for two minutes on the topic you choose using words, phrases, ideas, descriptions, examples, stories, or any other information you would like to include.

CLONES/ CLONING	PLANETS	THE SPACE PROGRAM	IMPORTANT INVENTIONS
TECHNOLOGY	THE WORLD OF COMPUTERS	TIME TRAVEL	SCIENCE FICTION
GENES/ HEREDITY	TREES	FLOWERS	WILD ANIMALS
GERMS	RESEARCH/ EXPERIMENTS	SCIENTISTS	THE MEDICAL WORLD
HEALTH ISSUES	ELECTRICITY	ENERGY SOURCES	MACHINES

Name_____   Date_____

Talk About History

Talk for two minutes on the topic you choose using words, phrases, ideas, descriptions, examples, stories, or any other information you would like to include.

GEORGE WASHINGTON	ABRAHAM LINCOLN	FLAGS	WORLD WARS
CIVIL WARS	THE AMERICAN REVOLUTION	THE UNITED STATES OF AMERICA	JAPAN
MEXICO	CHINA	PIONEERS	NATIVE AMERICANS
METHODS OF TRANSPORTATION	THE INDUSTRIAL REVOLUTION	THE GREAT DEPRESSION	THE 1960s
THE 1950s	THE HISTORY OF AUTOMOBILES	OLD MOVIES	THE OLYMPIC GAMES

© McGraw-Hill Children's Publishing   IF87061 Brain Games

Name _____   Date _____

Popular Culture
Speak Your Mind

Top Ten Talk

Talk for two minutes on your top ten, all-time favorites in the topics on these cards using words, phrases, ideas, descriptions, examples, stories, or any other information you would like to include.

TOP TEN COLLEGES	TOP TEN SONGS	TOP TEN MOVIES	TOP TEN BOOKS
TOP TEN SPORTS TEAMS	TOP TEN SPORTS	TOP TEN CITIES	TOP TEN STATES
TOP TEN COUNTRIES	TOP TEN FOODS	TOP TEN GAMES	TOP TEN HOBBIES
TOP TEN JOBS	TOP TEN THINGS TO STUDY	TOP TEN VACATION SPOTS	TOP TEN ANIMALS
TOP TEN RESTAURANTS	TOP TEN ACTORS/ ACTRESSES	TOP TEN SINGERS/ SINGING GROUPS	TOP TEN STORES

© McGraw-Hill Children's Publishing   IF87061 Brain Games

Name_____ Date_____

Language Arts
Speak Your Mind

Abstractly Speaking

Talk for two minutes on the abstract noun you choose using words, phrases, ideas, descriptions, examples, stories, or any other information you would like to include.

DEMOCRACY	RESPONSIBILITY	RESPECT	MORALS
COMMUNITY	COMMUNICATION	FRIENDSHIP	HUMOR
PRIDE	SYMPATHY	COURAGE	WISDOM
IMAGINATION	EXCITEMENT	PATRIOTISM	KINDNESS
GOSSIP	HAPPINESS	ANGER	FEAR

Name_____ Date_____

Controversy

Give two minutes worth of your ideas and opinions on the controversy you choose using words, phrases, descriptions, examples, stories, or any other information you like.

Year-round schools vs. traditional schedule schools	Home schooling vs. private schools vs. public schools	Who has a harder time in life— boys or girls?	What is the proper punishment for a child criminal?
Should kids get an allowance?	What chores should kids do at home?	How do you decide if a movie is appropriate for children?	Is there too much sex and violence on television?
How much TV watching is too much?	Should both parents work outside of the home?	How can you best help homeless and hungry families?	Should kids have a bedtime?
Should you have to eat everything on your plate at a meal?	What is a good time for a teenager's curfew?	Should parents forbid their kids from hanging out with "bad influences"?	Would kids learn more or less if no grades were given in school?
Are there any school subjects kids shouldn't have to take?	What animal makes the best pet?	How old should you be to do the following: date, get a job, wear make-up, get married?	Should families eat at least one meal together each day?

Instructions: Know Your Neighbor

Players: Entire class

Materials: Game cards, dry erase board, markers, scissors

Object: Along with your fellow team members, write true statements about the members of your neighboring team.

Rules:

1. Divide the class into Team A and Team B. Select a team leader for each team.
2. Select one game card from the *Know Your Neighbor* series. Make two copies of the card you selected and give one copy to the team leader of each team. Ask each team leader to cut the team's game card into 20 minicards by cutting along the dotted lines. Ask team leaders to distribute one minicard to each person on his or her team. (Depending on the size of your class, some minicards may not be used.)
3. Now all players on both teams try to make their statements true by filling in the name of one student from the opposing team. If a player believes no name will make his or her mini-card statement true, he or she should fill in the blank with the words "no one."
4. Beginning with the team leader, require each member of Team A to read his or her minicard statement aloud. After each statement is read, the person referred to must indicate whether or not the player from Team A has created a true statement. For each true statement created, Team A earns one point.
5. Now allow Team B players to read their minicard statements. Team B earns one point for each true minicard statement created. The team with the most points wins.

Know Your Neighbor

Student Scientists

_____ knows what 0° Celsius equals in Fahrenheit.

_____ owns a pet rodent.

_____ owns a pet reptile.

_____ has seen an alligator in the wild.

_____ has never been to a zoo.

_____ has planted a vegetable garden.

_____ has planted flowers.

_____ has planted a tree.

_____ has picked up and thrown away someone else's garbage.

_____ has been to a science or technology museum.

_____ has flown on a plane.

_____ uses an alternative energy source at home (e.g., solar, wind turbine, geothermal heat).

_____ has been stung by a bee.

_____ knows how many centimeters are in a meter.

_____ has started a bug collection.

_____ has never been to a beach.

_____ has hiked in the mountains.

_____ has swum in a river or lake.

Name_____   Date _____

Social Studies
Know Your Neighbor

Places I've Been

_____ has lived in or visited Mexico.

_____ has lived in or visited Canada.

_____ has lived in or visited Washington, D.C.

_____ has lived in or visited a European country.

_____ has visited Mount Vernon.

_____ has lived in or visited Hollywood.

_____ has lived in or visited a South American country.

_____ has lived in or visited San Francisco's Chinatown.

_____ has lived in or visited Idaho.

_____ has lived in or visited Denver, Colorado.

_____ has visited Disneyland.

_____ has lived in or visited Miami, Florida.

_____ has lived in or visited a Native American reservation.

_____ has visited Yosemite.

_____ has visited Niagara Falls.

_____ has visited Mt. Rushmore.

_____ has lived in or visited Alaska.

_____ has lived in a town bordering a river.

© McGraw-Hill Children's Publishing   IF87061 *Brain Games*

Know Your Neighbor

A Number of Things

_____ has more than $100 in a savings account.

_____ has exactly two brothers.

_____ has no sisters.

_____ has three or more living grandparents.

_____ has no more than one sibling.

_____ has at least five relatives who live within 100 miles of home.

_____ knows the names of the five Great Lakes.

_____ can name three major rivers in the United States.

_____ can name the seven continents.

_____ has flown on a plane more than twice.

_____ owns six or more pairs of jeans.

_____ has attended two or more professional sporting events.

_____ owns five or more pets.

_____ owns ten or more CDs.

_____ has read at least seven books this year.

_____ has more than six cousins.

_____ has moved three or more times.

_____ can name the Three Stooges.

Name _____ Date _____

Language Arts: Know Your Neighbor

Bookworms

_____ knows the title of one Shel Silverstein book.

_____ has read the book or seen the movie *Old Yeller*.

_____ has read *The Emperor's New Clothes*.

_____ has read *Charlotte's Web*.

_____ has seen the movie version of *The Wizard of OZ*.

_____ owns a *Winnie the Pooh* book.

_____ has read one or more of the *Little House* books.

_____ knows which bear in *Goldilocks* has cold porridge.

_____ knows what kind of an animal Babar is.

_____ can name one story about a frog.

_____ knows what kind of animal Paddington is.

_____ has read a Beverly Cleary book.

_____ has read a Judy Blume book.

_____ owns at least ten picture books.

_____ can recite a full Mother Goose rhyme.

_____ can give the titles of at least two Dr. Seuss stories.

_____ has seen the movie version of *The Red Balloon*.

_____ has read *The Little Prince*.

Know Your Neighbor

This Modern World

_____ owns his or her own camera.

_____ usually uses a mechanical pencil.

_____ owns a hand-held CD player.

_____ owns a hand-held computer game.

_____ has used a power tool.

_____ owns a solar-powered calculator.

_____ owns a battery-operated alarm clock.

_____ has a computer at home.

_____ has taken a machine apart.

_____ has a food processor at home.

_____ has a bread maker at home.

_____ has an espresso machine at home.

_____ has played an electric keyboard or electric guitar.

_____ owns a DVD player.

_____ has ridden in a car with a computer mapping system.

_____ has ridden in a car built in the 21st century.

_____ has an Internet connection at home.

_____ has a relative who has a pacemaker or artificial limb.

Instructions

Let Me Explain

Players: Entire class

Materials: Game cards, scissors

Goal: Students guess the identity of twenty words and phrases by their descriptions

Rules:

1. Select a game card from the *Let Me Explain* series. Make five copies of the game card.
2. Divide the class into five groups. Give each group a copy of the game card. Have a student cut the game card apart to create individual word or number cards. Have each group place their cards facedown in a single stack.
3. A player from each group will select a card. He or she will then give the group clues about the word or number shown on the card. The player may not use any form of the word or number to create clues.
4. When a teammate guesses the word or number, the card is placed in a discard pile. Then the next player chooses a card.
5. Play continues until each player in the circle has had a chance to draw a card from the stack and describe to teammates what is written on the card.

Name _____ Date _____

Let Me Explain

Parts and Pieces

Give your teammates clues until they correctly guess the word. Each word describes a part or piece of a machine.

SPRING	SOCKET	HAMMER	NAIL
TUBE	BLADE	WASHER	PIN
WHEEL	GEAR	CORD	WIRE
PLUG	HANDLE	LEVER	SWITCH
FILTER	BELT	BUTTON	DIAL

History of Communication

Give clues until your teammates guess the invention.

TELEVISION	TELEPHONE	COMPUTER	INTERNET
PRINTING PRESS	BOOKS	TYPEWRITER	TAPE RECORDER
CAMCORDER	VCR	MOVIE	RADIO
CELL PHONE	TELECONFERENCE	LONG DISTANCE LEARNING	DVD
COMPACT DISC	CHAT ROOM	E-MAIL	FAX MACHINE

Guess My Number

Get your teammates to guess the number on the card without using the number or *any of its digits* in your clues.

11	234	578	98
986	33	45	67
3,459	9,834	6,758	2,309
8	56	89	23
17	76	222	943

Name_____ Date_____

Language Arts

Let Me Explain

Adjective Answers

Get your teammates to guess the adjectives by giving clues that do not include any form of the word on the card.

BLUE	FIVE	SLOW	YELLOW
COLORFUL	ARTISTIC	TALENTED	OLD
PROUD	PRETTY	SMART	ANGRY
HAPPY	CRANKY	INTERESTING	EXPENSIVE
ELEGANT	COLD	SCARY	LOUD

Name _____ Date _____

Places to Go, Things to Do
Use clues to help your teammates guess the place or event named on the card.

CONCERT HALL	CIRCUS	PARK	ZOO
STADIUM	SKATING RINK	ARENA	AMUSEMENT PARK
FAIR	MUSEUM	MOVIE THEATER	VIDEO ARCADE
MALL	HIKING TRAIL	CAMPGROUND	BEACH
SKI RESORT	MOUNTAINS	DESERT	THEATER

© McGraw-Hill Children's Publishing   IF87061 *Brain Games*

Instructions

Story Add-Ons

Players: Entire class

Materials: Game card, scissors, tape, butcher paper, markers

Goal: Students cooperate with other classmates to write a single creative and coherent class story.

Rules:
1. Select a game card from the *Story Add-Ons* series.
2. Cut the cards along the black lines to create individual word cards.
3. Shuffle the word cards and distribute one to each student in the class. It is not necessary to use all cards if there are fewer than thirty students in your class.
4. Near the top of the butcher paper, write the story-starter sentence from the game card you chose.
5. Challenge each student in the class to add a sentence to the story. The sentence must contain the word on the card he or she was given. Students may wish to volunteer to add a sentence when the topic of their word card seems to fit the storyline. Continue play until all students have added their sentences.
6. When a word could be used as more than one part of speech, the student must use it in the way indicated on the card. Capitalized words must be used at the beginnings of sentences. Lower-cased words may not be used at the beginnings of sentences. Student sentences must be logical and coherent additions to the story. The last sentence should create a sensible conclusion.

Name_____ Date_____

Science Stories

Story-Starter: Professor Fields was certain his new concoction would somehow benefit mankind.

Scientists noun	laboratory noun	He noun	households noun	benefit noun
Working verb	discovered verb	helped verb	improves verb	were verb
amazing adjective	The adjective	a adjective	alarming adjective	surprising adjective
extremely adverb	newly adverb	quite adverb	too adverb	Hysterically adverb
Before preposition	until preposition	over preposition	beyond preposition	In preposition
and conjunction	While conjunction	because conjunction	that conjunction	Wow! interjection

Name_____ Date_____

Social Studies

Story Add-Ons

Political Play

Story-Starter: The children of Harding Elementary finally decided to approach their town's mayor about the unsightly litter problem on Main Street.

politician	President	Senator	mayor	judge
noun	noun	noun	noun	noun
revoked	overruled	vetoed	angered	pleased
verb	verb	verb	verb	verb
necessary	Legal	agitated	intelligent	happy
adjective	adjective	adjective	adjective	adjective
Soon	slowly	joyously	never	always
adverb	adverb	adverb	adverb	adverb
About	across	after	before	next to
preposition	preposition	preposition	preposition	preposition
but	or	neither nor	Before	for
conjunction	conjunction	conjunction	conjunction	conjunction

© McGraw-Hill Children's Publishing

Numbers in the Kitchen

Story-Starter: Sally and her grandma decided to make a special dessert for the family on Valentine's Day.

recipe	batch	Grandma Miller	kitchen	dozen
noun	noun	noun	noun	noun
Cut	Serve	bake	mix	eat
verb	verb	verb	verb	verb
Half	one-third	delicious	huge	four
adjective	adjective	adjective	adjective	adjective
hardly	Sometimes	gently	nicely	not
adverb	adverb	adverb	adverb	adverb
without	Under	past	onto	during
preposition	preposition	preposition	preposition	preposition
If	rather than	Since	though	When
conjunction	conjunction	conjunction	conjunction	conjunction

Storytellers

Story-Starter: It was a quiet, rainy afternoon at youth camp.

storyteller	Queen	hero	guy	girl
noun	noun	noun	noun	noun
get	ride	Run	scare	trip
verb	verb	verb	verb	verb
A	The	bad	good	poor
adjective	adjective	adjective	adjective	adjective
Once	happily	always	ever	absolutely
adverb	adverb	adverb	adverb	adverb
upon	after	throughout	toward	under
preposition	preposition	preposition	preposition	preposition
and	either or	for	Cool!	Ouch!
conjunction	conjunction	conjunction	interjection	interjection

Name_____ Date_____

Language Arts
Story Add-Ons

Circus Performers

Story-Starter: Kerry wasn't sure he would enjoy the Pleasantville People's Circus since it featured absolutely no animals.

Clowns	Dancers	magicians	actors	singers
noun	noun	noun	noun	noun
painting	dancing	sings	acts	smiles
verb	verb	verb	verb	verb
clumsy	Silly	Wild	shocking	gorgeous
adjective	adjective	adjective	adjective	adjective
beautifully	gracefully	never	accidentally	intentionally
adverb	adverb	adverb	adverb	adverb
around	opposite	near	beyond	Behind
preposition	preposition	preposition	preposition	preposition
but	so	for	Hurray!	Gasp
conjunction	conjunction	conjunction	interjection	interjection

© McGraw-Hill Children's Publishing

Instructions

Sentence Sense

Players: Entire class

Materials: Game cards, scissors

Goal: Match sentence fragments to create complete sentences.

Rules:
1. Select a game card from the *Sentence Sense* series.
2. Reproduce and distribute one card to each of five teams.
3. One team member on each team cuts along the black lines to create individual sentence fragment cards.
4. All teams begin play at once. Players on each team work together to connect sentence fragment pairs into sensible sentences. When all sentence fragments have been matched, the team calls out, *Sentence Sense*.
5. The first team to call out *Sentence Sense* must check their answers with you. If all of their sentence fragments have been connected correctly, they are the winning team.

Answer Key
Sentence Sense

Sentence fragments should combine to form twelve sentences per game card. The sentences are numbered here for clarity, but you may list them in any order as long as the fragments are combined to create the sentences indicated.

Here's the Rub:
1. Natural rubber is secreted from certain plants in the form of latex particles suspended in water. 2. South American countries have made use of natural rubbers for centuries. 3. Most rubber compounds used today are man-made. 4. Rubber claimed its name when a British scientist named Joseph Priestly observed that it could rub out pencil marks. 5. Rubber's ability to bounce made it a novelty in Europe after Christopher Columbus introduced it to the continent. 6. Natural rubber becomes soft and sticky when hot and brittle when cold if not mixed with other chemicals. 7. In 1839, Charles Goodyear produced a useful rubber by heating it with sulfur. 8. Most rubber mixtures today contain no more than 60% rubber. 9. Rubber became a valuable commodity with the rise of the automotive industry. 10. Most natural rubber today comes from commercial tree farms throughout Asia. 11. Synthetic rubber became popular during World War II. 12. Although many rubber products are made, over fifty percent of rubber today is used in the production of tires.

Picturing History:
1. Mathew Brady was born in the early 1800s. 2. Mathew Brady was always interested in art. 3. Mathew Brady learned to take pictures with one of the world's earliest versions of the camera. 4. Rich people in New York City went to Mathew Brady's studio to have their photographs taken. 5. Mathew Brady liked to take pictures of famous Americans. 6. Mathew Brady took pictures of American authors, artists, inventors, and presidents. 7. During the Civil War, Mathew Brady used his own money to record the war in pictures. 8. Mathew Brady took pictures of Edgar Allan Poe, Andrew Jackson, and Abraham Lincoln. 9. When the Civil War ended, the United States government did not want to pay Mathew Brady for his war pictures. 10. Mathew Brady once said, "the camera is the eye of history." 11. After the Civil War, Mathew Brady went bankrupt. 12. Mathew Brady died in poverty.

Engineering and Design:
1. George Ferris was an engineer who lived in the 1800s. 2. George Ferris designed and built railroad bridges. 3. In 1885, George Ferris designed a massive rotating wheel. 4. Five years after he designed it, George Ferris began building his wheel using steel girders. 5. The wheel was approximately 260 feet high. 6. The wheel was displayed at the World's Columbian Exposition in Chicago in 1893. 7. The wheel had thirty-six cars with each car seating sixty people. 8. People paid fifty cents to ride the first Ferris Wheel. 9. George Ferris's massive wheel was powered by two one-thousand horsepower steam engines. 10. Modern Ferris wheels are powered by electricity. 11. Modern Ferris wheels are not usually as large as the original wheel. 12. George Ferris never patented his exciting new ride.

My Impression Is…:
1. Impressionism is the name given to much of the artwork of France in the late nineteenth century. 2. Claude Monet was a famous impressionistic painter. 3. Mary Cassatt was the only American artist associated with the impressionists. 4. Most impressionistic paintings depict landscapes. 5. Claude Monet painted several scenes more than once during different seasons, times of day, and weather conditions. 6. The impressionist Edgar Degas painted a series of ballerinas. 7. Vincent van Gogh is now a celebrated impressionist, but was not very successful in his own day. 8. Some impressionists painted using a series of dots called pointillism. 9. Paul Gauguin was a post-impressionist. 10. Impressionism greatly influenced modern art in the areas of color, freedom of brush strokes, and originality. 11. Edouard Manet's paintings contain some impressionistic traits. 12. Paul Cezanne, Camille Pissarro, and Alfred Sisley were impressionistic artists.

Here's the Rub

Natural rubber is	today are man-made.
South American countries have	commercial tree farms throughout Asia.
Most rubber compounds used	Joseph Priestly observed that it could rub out pencil marks.
Rubber's ability	produced a useful rubber by heating it with sulfur.
Natural rubber becomes	secreted from certain plants in the form of latex particles suspended in water.
In 1839, Charles Goodyear	popular during World War II.
Most rubber mixtures today contain	to bounce made it a novelty in Europe after Christopher Columbus introduced it to the continent.
Rubber became a valuable commodity with	soft and sticky when hot and brittle when cold if not mixed with other chemicals.
Rubber claimed its name when a British scientist named	rubber today is used in the production of tires.
Most natural rubber today comes from	made use of natural rubber for centuries.
Synthetic rubber became	no more than 60% rubber.
Although many rubber products are made, over fifty percent of	the rise of the automotive industry.

Picturing History

Mathew Brady was born	to take pictures of famous Americans.
Mathew Brady was always interested	in poverty.
Mathew Brady learned to take pictures with one of the world's	money to record the war in pictures.
Rich people in New York City went	in art.
Mathew Brady liked	Mathew Brady went bankrupt.
Mathew Brady took pictures of American	in the early 1800s.
During the Civil War, Mathew Brady used his own	of Edgar Allan Poe, Andrew Jackson, and Abraham Lincoln.
Mathew Brady took pictures	said, "the camera is the eye of history."
When the Civil War ended, the United States government did not	earliest versions of the camera.
Mathew Brady once	want to pay Mathew Brady for his war pictures.
After the Civil War	to Mathew Brady's studio to have their photographs taken.
Mathew Brady died	authors, artists, inventors, and presidents.

Engineering and Design

George Ferris was an engineer who lived	fifty cents to ride the first Ferris Wheel.
George Ferris designed and built	are powered by electricity.
In 1885, George Ferris designed a	in the 1800s.
Five years after he designed it,	the World's Columbian Exposition in Chicago in 1893.
The wheel	each car seating sixty people.
The wheel was displayed at	railroad bridges.
The wheel had thirty-six cars with	by two 1000-horsepower steam engines.
People paid	usually as large as the original wheel.
George Ferris's massive wheel was powered	patented his exciting new ride.
Modern Ferris Wheels	massive rotating wheel.
Modern Ferris Wheels are not	George Ferris began building his wheel using steel girders.
George Ferris never	was approximately 260 feet high.

Name _____ Date _____

Art Sentence Sense

My Impression Is...

Impressionism is the name	was the only American artist associated with the impressionists.
Claude Monet was a famous	celebrated impressionist, but was not very successful in his own day.
Mary Cassatt	given to much of the artwork of France in the late nineteenth century.
Most impressionistic paintings	influenced modern art in the areas of color, freedom of brush strokes, and originality.
Claude Monet painted several	impressionistic painter.
The impressionist	Alfred Sisley were impressionistic artists.
Vincent van Gogh is now a	depict landscapes.
Some impressionists painted using	some impressionistic traits.
Paul Gauguin was a	Edgar Degas painted a series of ballerinas.
Impressionism greatly	post-impressionist.
Edouard Manet's paintings contain	scenes more than once during different seasons, times of day, and weather conditions.
Paul Cezanne, Camille Pissarro, and	a series of tiny dots called pointillism.

Instructions: Ask the Experts

Players: Entire class

Materials: Game cards, scissors

Object: Consider and discuss traits of a healthy classroom community in a cooperative game atmosphere.

Note: This is a cooperative game that has no right or wrong answers and no winners or losers. All three game cards in *Ask the Experts* are to be used in the playing of a single game.

Rules:

1. Divide the class into four teams. Each team becomes a group of experts on an issue pertaining to a different set of healthy values for a cooperative classroom community.
2. Cut page 126 along the black lines to create four team title cards. Distribute one card to each team. Each team folds its title card along the dotted line so the card can stand on the team's table or desk.
3. Cut pages 127 and 128 along the black lines to create four interview cards. Give one interview card to each team. Teams should not hold the interview card with questions intended for themselves.
4. Each team chooses one person to be an interviewer and one person to be a respondent. Decide which team will begin play. The interviewer from that team asks the first question on his or her card of the team of experts to whom the question pertains.
5. The experts have three minutes to discuss the question and formulate an answer that reflects the characteristics of a healthy classroom community. The chosen respondent reports the team's response.
6. Continue play with another interviewer asking another team of experts for their opinion on another question from an interview card.
7. Continue play until all questions have been answered.
8. You may choose to involve the entire class in a dialogue about the answers given by each team.

Name ______________________ Date ______________

Cooperation

Ask the Experts

(Team Title Cards)

SHARING AND COOPERATING EXPERTS

RESPECT AND TOLERANCE EXPERTS

HONESTY AND TRUSTWORTHINESS EXPERTS

RESPONSIBILITY AND WORK ETHIC EXPERTS

Name _____ Date _____

Cooperation

Ask the Experts
(Interview Cards)

Interview Questions for the Sharing and Cooperating Experts:

1. Your best friend struggles with multiplication. One day in class, she passes you a note asking for a few answers to a test the class is taking. Will you share answers with your friend? Why might sharing test answers not be helpful to your friend?

2. One of the boys in your class does not have any art supplies. When you share your crayons or markers with him, a few always seem to mysteriously disappear. What should you do when he asks to borrow your art supplies again?

3. You are working with four other students on a group project that involves research, writing, speaking, and artwork. How might you ensure that every person in your group contributes to the project and works on areas in which he or she has special skills?

4. Sometimes the behaviors of just a few students in your class disrupt the entire class. How can you help disruptive students to work with the rest of the class to follow the teacher's directions?

--✂

Interview Questions for the Respect and Tolerance Experts:

1. One of your classmates is always left out of P.E. and recess activities. No one sits with the student at lunch or talks with him on breaks. How can you ensure that he is included in future activities?

2. The new student who arrived in your classroom yesterday has scars all over her body. It is difficult to act as if you do not notice her appearance. Would it be more respectful to ask the student about the history behind her scars or to try and ignore them?

3. Your best friend at school has just learned that your best friend at church is of a different ethnic background. Your school friend makes racial slurs against your church friend. How do you respond? Should you continue to be friends with someone who is prejudiced?

4. Your homeroom teacher is shy and inexperienced. Students in his class are often disruptive. How can you encourage your classmates to respect the new teacher? Is it your duty as a student to try and influence the behavior of other students or should you simply be sure your own behaviors are respectful?

Cooperation
Ask the Experts
(Interview Cards Continued)

**Interview Questions for the
Honesty and Trustworthiness Experts:**

1. A friend tells you he has started drinking alcohol from his parent's wine cabinet after school and on weekends. Your friend says he realizes drinking is not a good idea, so he has promised to quit immediately. He begs you not to tell anyone his secret. Will you tell anyone? If so, whom?
2. You promised to help a classmate study for a test on Saturday. Now you find out your grandmother is coming from out of state to visit for the entire weekend. What is the best way to resolve this dilemma?
3. Your friend asks you how you like her new haircut. The truth is, you don't. What do you say?
4. Your teacher has decided to let some students work on mathematics at their own pace. She has asked you to come up with a list of traits that would help her decide which students could be trusted to work on their own and correct their own work. What traits make someone trustworthy?

**Interview Questions for the
Responsibility and Work Ethic Experts:**

1. Think about some students in your class whom you consider responsible. What characteristics prove a person is responsible?
2. You have finished a social studies project early and done an excellent job on it. Your teacher asks you to help other students with their projects. You finished your project early thinking you could draw in your sketchbook. Is it fair for your teacher to ask you to help others with their projects when you worked hard to finish yours early so you could have some free time?
3. Your community is asking for volunteers to visit shut-ins and hospital patients. You are uncomfortable visiting with strangers, but you feel a responsibility to be a caring citizen of your community. Should you volunteer? If not, what other projects might you offer to do in your community instead?
4. Your band teacher has asked you to perform a solo during a concert. The music he gives you to play will require lots of practice at home every night from now until the concert in two months. What are some benefits you might gain from putting that much extra time and work into playing your instrument? What benefits might you gain from attending the concert?

© McGraw-Hill Children's Publishing   IF87061 Brain Games